Halkidiki

The secret Paradise of Greece

Chalkidiki

Ein Paradies reich an Geheimnissen

Walking/Wandern

Financed by the European Union, 2nd C.S.F.
(Regional Development European Fund)
Operational Programme of Hellenic Tourism Organisation

Routes in Kassandra — ***Routen auf Kassandra***

1. Sani-Beach - Sani Bird Sanctuary/*Sani Vogelschutzgebiet*
2. Sani - Sani Camping - Siviri
3. Possidi/*Possidi*
4. Polychrono - Turtles (*Schildkrötenteich*) - Polychrono
5. Kriopigi - Kassandrino - Kriopigi
6. Hanioti - Fire Tower (*Feuerwachturm*) - Hanioti

Routes in Sithonia — ***Routen auf Sithonia***

7. Elia Beach - Ag. Pavlos - Petros - Elia Beach
8. Nikiti - Ag. Nikolaos - Nikiti
9. Neos Marmaras - Parthenonas - Neos Marmaras
10. Porto Carras - Vineyards (*Weinberge*)
11. Porto Koufo - Kapros - Porto Koufo
12. Sikia - Sikia

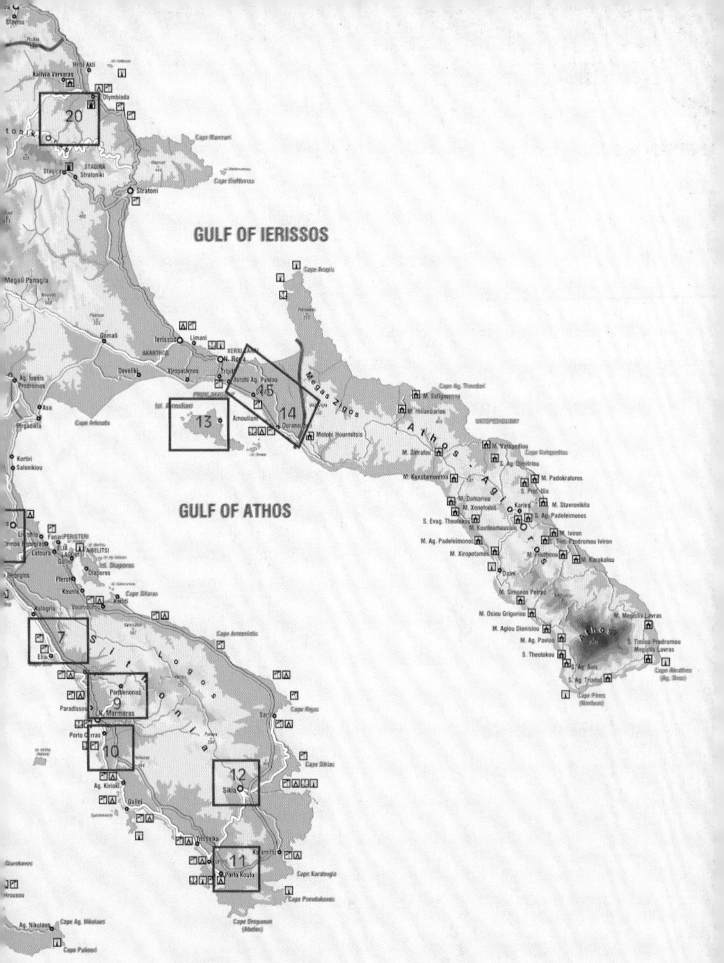

Routes in Athos / *Routen auf Athos*

13. Amouliani Island *Insel Amouliani*
14. Ouranoupolis - Mt. Athos Border - Ouranoupolis
    Ouranoupolis - Berg Athos Grenze - Ouranoupolis
15. Ouranoupolis - Hotels

Routes in Holomondas Mountains *Routen im Holomondas Gebirge*

16. Polygiros - Tsoukalas - Polygiros
17. Taxiarchis - Vrastama
18. Vrastama - Ag. Efthimios
19. Holomondas - Paleochora
20. **Olympiada** - circular route (*Rundwanderung*)

20 Walks in Halkidiki
Wanderrouten auf Chalkidiki

David Ramshaw

This book is published by the Halkidiki Hotel Association at the address shown below.

Herausgegeben von der Chalkidiki Hotel Vereinigung (Adresse siehe unten).

If you wish to order a copy of this book please contact:

Weitere Exemplare sind unter folgender Anschrift erhältlich:

33, G. Papandreou St.,
54646 Thessaloniki
Greece.

Tel.Nr.: 0030/31/429020
Fax : 0030/31/429021
e-mail:
halkidiki-assoc@the.forthnet.gr
http://www.halkidiki-hotels.gr

In the U.K the book can be ordered from the author:

In Großbritanien kann das Buch beim Autor bestellt werden.

David Ramshaw,
13 Beaver Road,
Carlisle, Cumbria
CA2 7PS - England

Tel: 0044/1228/543314
e-mail: P3pub@aol.com

The selection of the walking routes and the production of this book was co-ordinated by:

Die Auswahl der Wanderungen und die Zusammenstellung dieses Buchs erfolgte unter Koordination von:

A la carte Travel
19, Pan. Korifinis St.,
632 00 Nea Moudania
Greece

Tel. 0030/373/25261
Fax 0030/373/25288
e-mail: alacarte@mail.otenet.gr
http://www.alacarte-travel.com

German translation from the English by Kallia Kotsovolos.

Übersetzt aus dem Englischen von Kallia Kotsovolos.

Printed by Art Center
36, Stromnitsis St.,
54248 Thessaloniki, Greece

Tel. 0030/31/310356
Fax 0030/31/318672
e-mail: atcent@otenet.gr

Cover, Red Design
42, Vas. Georgiou St.,
546 40 Thessaloniki, Greece

Tel. 0030/31/842787
Fax 0030/31/862534
e-mail: redd@otenet.gr

ISBN 0 9522098 9 6
British Library Cataloguing in Publication Data
A catalogue record for this book is available from the British Library.

Das Buch ist im Veröffentlichungsverzeichnis der Britischen Bibliothek registriert.

Acknowledgements
Vorwort

My grateful thanks go to all those people who have helped me to complete this book. In particular to Andreas Birner and Maria Kyrlidou of A La Carte Travel in Nea Moudania for getting me involved in the Halkidiki Hiking Programme, after a chance meeting on holiday at Sani Beach. Andreas and Maria are responsible to the Halkidiki Hotel Association for the whole project. Without their help, guidance and hospitality the book would not have been possible.

Grateful thanks also to the Greek National Tourist Organisation and the Halkidiki Hotel Association for entrusting me with the research of the routes, the writing of the book and of course for funding its publication.

Thanks also to my good friends, Günther and Karin Hüttner who accompanied me and guided me on many of the routes. Their valuable local knowledge was much appreciated. Last but not least, my thanks go to my wife and family, who have all had to take on extra responsibilities during my long absence from home to research and write the book.

Mein herzlicher Dank gilt allen denen, die mir bei der Verwirklichung dieses Buches geholfen haben. Insbesondere danke ich Andreas Birner und Maria Kyrlidou von A La Carte Travel in Nea Moudania, die mich nach unserer zufälligen Begegnung während meiner Ferien im Sani Beach Hotel, am Chalkidiki Wanderprogramm beteiligt haben. Andreas und Maria sind zuständig und verantwortlich für das ganze Projekt. Ohne ihre Hilfe, Beratung und Gastfreundschaft wäre dieses Buch nicht entstanden.

Ferner danke ich der Griechischen Zentrale für Fremdenverkehr und der Chalkidiki Hotel Vereinigung, die mir das Erforschen der Routen und das Schreiben des Buches anvertraut haben und die darüber hinaus die Veröffentlichung des Buches finanziert haben.

Meinen guten Freunden Günther und Karin Hüttner sei an dieser Stelle auch gedankt. Sie haben mich auf vielen Routen begleitet und geführt, wobei ihre wertvollen Kenntnisse von der Region von großem Nutzen waren.

Zum Schluß danke ich noch meiner Ehefrau und Familie, die während meiner langen Abwesenheit von zu Hause mit zusätzlichen Aufgaben verpflichtet waren.

Welcome to Halkidiki
Willkommen auf Chalkidiki

Dear friends of Greece,
It is a great pleasure for me to welcome you as a "Xenos", a guest, here in Greece. As a representative of the EOT, the Hellenic Tourism Organisation, I welcome particularly the initiative of the Halkidiki Hotel Association, who have now established a Hiking programme for our guests. I am delighted, to wish you good reading for the new walking guide, and nice walks in Poseidons kingdom!

Liebe Griechenland - Freunde,
Mit besonderer Freude heiße ich Sie als *xenos*, bzw. Gast, hier in Griechenland willkommen. Als Vertreter der EOT, der griechischen Zentrale für Fremdenverkehr, begrüße ich insbesondere die Initiative der Chalkidiki Hotel Association, dieses Wanderprogramm für unsere Gäste zu verwirklichen. Demnach wünsche ich Ihnen viel Vergnügen beim Lesen dieser Lektüre und natürlich viel Freude beim Wandern.

Giannakopoulos Evgenios **Secretary General. EOT**

Dear guest, our new walking guide describes 20 different walking routes. You will find the trident symbol at the hotel doors, in brochures and on the way-markers. It is no accident, that we choose the trident as a waymarker. Halkidiki, with its three prongs piercing into the Aegean Sea, looks from above like Poseidon's trident.
The local people call Halkidiki *the green garden of Greece*, due to its pine and oak forests on the hills, the vineyards and the cornfields, which often extend as far as the water's edge.
The best way to explore this lovely countryside is on foot. We have recently cleared and way-marked 20 routes on Kassandra, Sithonia, Athos and Holomondas.
They give you the best opportunity to get to know the people, their history, and the beauty of this unspoilt region. In this regard, welcome to Halkidiki.

Liebe Gäste, unser neuer Wanderführer beschreibt 20 verschiedene Wanderrouten. Sie werden das Dreizacksymbol an Hoteltüren, in Broschüren und auf den Wegweisern antreffen. Die Wahl des Dreizacks als Wegweiser ist nicht zufällig, denn Chalkidiki, mit seinen drei Ausläufern, die in die Ägäis ragen, sieht wie der Dreizack von Poseidon aus.
Wegen der Kiefern- und Eichenwälder auf den Bergen, sowie den Weinbergen und Weizenfeldern, die bis ans Meer reichen, wird Chalkidiki von den Einheimischen *der grüne Garten Griechenlands* genannt.
Am besten erschließen Sie diese wunderschöne Landschaft zu Fuß. Wir haben kürzlich 20 Routen auf Kassandra, Sithonia Holomondas und Athos freigelegt und ausgeschildert. Auf diese Weise lernen Sie Land und Leute, und die unberührte Natur dieser Region kennen. In diesem Sinne also, herzlich Willkommen auf Chalkidiki.

Dr. Andreas Andreadis
President of the Halkidiki Hotel Association

Contents Inhalt Page/Seite

Welcome to Halkidiki ***Wilkommen auf Chalkidiki***

Acknowledgements ***Vorwort***

Introduction ***Einleitung***

Routes in Kassandra ***Routen auf Kassandra***

1.	Sani-Beach - Sani Bird Sanctuary/*Sani Vogelschutzgebiet*	16
2.	Sani - Sani Camping - Siviri	21
3.	Possidi/*Possidi*	28
4.	Polychrono - Turtles (*Schildkrötenteich*) - Polychrono	33
5.	Kriopigi - Kassandrino - Kriopigi	38
6.	Hanioti - Fire Tower (*Feuerwachturm*) - Hanioti	43

Routes in Sithonia ***Routen auf Sithonia***

7.	Elia Beach - Ag. Pavlos - Petros - Elia Beach	51
8.	Nikiti - Ag. Nikolaos - Nikiti	55
9.	Neos Marmaras - Parthenonas - Neos Marmaras	60
10.	Porto Carras - Vineyards (*Weinberge*)	66
11.	Porto Koufo - Kapros - Porto Koufo	72
12.	Sikia - Sikia	76

Routes in Athos ***Routen auf Athos***

13.	Amouliani Island *Insel Amouliani*	87
14.	Ouranoupolis - Mt. Athos Border - Ouranoupolis *Ouranoupolis - Berg Athos Grenze - Ouranoupolis*	92
15.	Ouranoupolis - Hotels	96

Routes in Holomondas Mountains ***Routen im Holomondas Gebirge***

16.	Polygiros - Tsoukalas - Polygiros	101
17.	Taxiarchis - Vrastama	105
18.	Vrastama - Ag. Efthimios	111
19.	Holomondas - Paleochora	119
20.	**Olympiada** - circular route (*Rundwanderung*)	123

Fishing boats in Ouranoupolis
Fischerboote in Ouranoupolis

Introduction
Einleitung

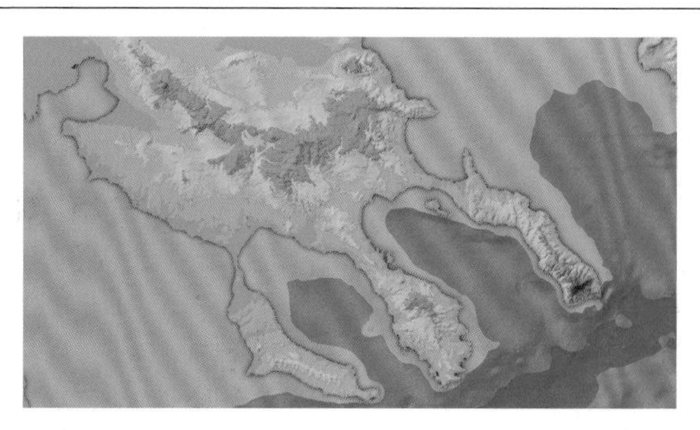

Halkidiki seen from space

Halkidiki is the three-pronged peninsula, which extends southward into the Aegean Sea from the centre of Macedonia. As a result of its shape and the close proximity of the sea, Halkidiki benefits from a mild climate and has the longest coastline on mainland Greece.

This walking guide has been written to fulfill a growing need. Many of the increasing number of English and German visitors to the area, particularly in Spring and Autumn, wish to enjoy a more active holiday and to explore the countryside on foot. This guide describes twenty routes in Halkidiki that have been recently cleared and way-marked thus:

Chalkidiki aus dem All

Calkidiki ist die dreizackförmige Halbinsel, die von Zentral-mazedonien südwärts in die Ägäische See ausläuft. Aufgrund ihrer eigenartigen Form und unmittelbaren Nähe zum Meer verfügt Chalkidiki über mildes Klima und weist die längste Küstenstrecke auf dem griechischen Festland auf.

Der zunehmenden Nachfrage folgend wurde dieser Wanderführer verfaßt. Die Anzahl der Besucher aus England und Deutschland wächst seit Jahren ständig, und besonders jene, die die Region im Frühling oder Herbst besuchen, bevorzugen einen aktiveren Ferienaufenthalt und möchten die Landschaft zu Fuß erschließen.

Dieser Wanderführer beschreibt zwanzig Wanderrouten auf Chalkidiki, die kürzlich freigelegt wurden und wie links beschildert sind :

Sie werden auf den Wanderwegen auf kleine,

Along the route the way will be marked either by *Poseidon* symbols (black on white) nailed to trees etc. or red paint spray on rocks as shown below.

Showing the way with trident markers

Although this book is primarily a walking guide, it also gives an insight into the people, their origins, history, and the nature of the land, which they inhabit.

The following symbols will be used on the maps and in the text.

 Route information

 Historical information

 Flora and fauna

 Animal world

 Viewpoint

Start Start of walk

schwarzweiße Wegweiser treffen, die an Bäumen o.ä. befestigt sind, und den Dreizack von Poseidon darstellen, z.T. ist der Weg auch mit roter Farbe auf Felsen und Steinen gekennzeichnet (siehe Bild unten). Obwohl diese Broschüre in erster Linie einen Wanderführer darstellt, haben

Der Dreizack dient als Wegmarkierung

wir uns bemüht auch etwas Informationen über die Bewohner der Chalkidiki, ihre Herkunft und Geschichte, und die Besonderheiten der Region die sie bewohnen, aufzunehmen.

Folgende Zeichen werden in den Wegbeschreibungen und auf den Landkarten benutzt : (Zeichenerklärung)

 Wegbeschreibung

 Historische Informationen

 Flora und Fauna

 Tierwelt

 Aussichtspunkt

 Beginn der Wanderung

The routes cover a wide area of the peninsula:
Routes 1-6 are in Kassandra, the most westerly prong of the peninsula.
Routes 7-12 are in Sithonia, the central prong, which is a more rugged terrain than Kassandra.
Routes 13-15 are found at the neck of the Athos prong, which consists of flatter terrain linking two gulfs of the Aegean Sea.
Routes 16-19 lie in the foothills of Mt. Holomondas, near Polygiros.
Route 20 lies on its own in the area of Olympiada.

Good footwear is necessary for all of the routes. In most situations strong shoes or trainers will suffice. When wet, however, summer walking boots are recommended, particularly for one or two of the longer routes, and those that involve some rock scrambling. The conditions should never be worse than walking the English Lakes, or the Black Forest in a normal summer, except on the odd occasion when torrential downpours can occur. Generally the conditions are dry and warm, even in March and October and you are more likely to need suncream than a cagoule. January is usually a good month for walking, with many crisp sunny days and occasional snow in the Holomondas mountains.

A Brief History of the Area.

Halkidiki features often in Greek mythology and was the site of two important cities in Classical Greek times. The area was good for agriculture and there was the added attraction of its mineral

Die Wanderrouten erstrecken sich über einen großen Teil der Halbinsel :
Die Routen 1 - 6 befinden sich auf Kassandra, dem westlichen Ausläufer der Halbinsel.
Die Routen 7 - 12 auf Sithonia, dem mittleren Ausläufer, wo die Landschaft gebirgiger ist als auf Kassandra.
Die Routen 13 - 15 liegen auf dem frei zugänglichen Teil der Halbinsel Athos.
Hier treffen der Golf von Agion Oros und der Golf von Ierissos aufeinander.
Die Routen 16 - 19 verlaufen an den Flanken des Holomondas Gebirges, bei Polygiros.
Die Route 20 führt durch die Umgebung des Dorfes Olympiada.
Für alle Routen ist gutes Schuhwerk erforderlich. In den meisten Fällen genügen aber auch geschlossene Schuhe oder Sportschuhe. Bei Regenwetter empfehle ich Ihnen allerdings, leichte Wanderschuhe zu tragen, besonders für längere Strecken oder auf Wanderungen die über felsiges Gelände führen.
Grundsätzlich sind die Wetter- und Wanderbedingungen auf Chalkidiki im Frühjahr, Herbst und Winter ähnlich den Englischen Seen oder dem Schwarzwald, mit Ausnahme einiger weniger Fälle, wo es für kurze Zeit in Strömen regnen kann.
Im Allgemeinen ist das Wetter trocken und warm, sogar im März und im Oktober, so daß Sie eher eine Sonnenschutzcreme benötigen als einen Anorak. Der Januar ist ebenfalls gut zum Wandern geeignet. Es ist trocken und sonnig, und vielleicht liegt sogar etwas Schnee im Holomondas Gebirge.

wealth, from which a prosperous mining industry gradually developed. The Thraceans, as the ancient Greeks named the local inhabitants, suffered many invasions and changes of allegiance over the centuries. After the Persian wars in the 5th century BC, the cities of the Thraceans, now known as the Chalcideans, became members of the Athenium Alliance. Unfortunately this failed to prevent further conflict and destruction, causing them, eventually, to set up their own league of cities for mutual protection.

An invasion by Sparta followed from which the league soon recovered, only to be eventually conquered by and incorporated into Greater Macedonia. In 168 BC new rulers arrived with the Roman invasion and the area was at relative peace until an invasion by Goths and Barbarians in 269 AD.

The Romans quickly re-asserted their power, but not before great destruction had occurred throughout the province. Peace reigned once more until the 6th century when Huns invaded the region.

Little is known of the succeeding two centuries as few records exist. From the 9th century onwards the monks who became established on Athos kept records. They describe many years of great upheaval, death and destruction. Despotic rulers, pirates, invaders, all took their toll on the local inhabitants. During the 15th and 16th century, when the Turks occupied Macedonia, many Greeks fled to Halkidiki and, with the development of

Geschichte der Region

Chalkidiki wird oft in der griechischen Mythologie erwähnt. Zwei der wichtigsten Städte in der Antike befanden sich auf Chalkidiki. Die Region eignete sich hervorragend für den landwirtschaftlichen Anbau und ihr enormer Reichtum an Erzen führte zur frühen Entwicklung der Erzindustrie.

Die Thrakier, so wurden die Bewohner von den alten Griechen benannt, erlitten über die Jahrhunderte hinweg mehrere, zerstörende Invasionen und Besetzungen. Nach den Persischen Kriegen im 5.Jahrhundert v.Chr. wurden die Städte der Thrakier, der heutigen Bewohner Chalkidikis, Mitglieder im Athener Bund.

Das bewahrte sie aber trotzdem nicht vor weiteren Überfällen und Zerstörungen, und führte schließlich dazu, daß sie sich zu einem eigenen Bündnis zusammenschlossen, um sich gegenseitigen Schutz zu gewähren. Sie überlebten zwar den darauffolgenden Angriff der Spartaner, wurden aber dennoch vom Mazedonischen Reich erobert und unterworfen.

168 v.Chr. wurden sie von den Römern besetzt. Die neuen Herrscher sorgten für Frieden, der bis zu der Invasion der Goten und Barbaren im Jahre 366 v.Chr. anhielt.

Die Römer kamen wieder schnell an die Macht, doch das Land büßte mit verheerenden Zerstörungen. Es kehrte wieder Frieden ein, bis die Hunen im 6. Jahrhundert einmarschierten.

Man erfährt nur wenig über die darauffolgenden zwei Jahrhunderte, da nur wenige schriftliche Aufzeichnungen erhalten sind. Erst ab dem 9.Jahrhundert werden von

the mining industry, relative calm ensued under Turkish domination for more than two centuries. In the early 19th century the villages of Halkidiki were formed into three federations or co-operatives, supervised by a representative of the Turkish Government. They paid their taxes direct to Constantinople. However, in 1821 there was an uprising against the small Turkish garrisons administering the area, triggered by the refusal of many Halkidikans to be conscripted into the Turkish Army. This led to another period of great unrest, which lasted through two Balkan wars. Peace finally came to the area in 1912 when the Greek rebels of Halkidiki ejected the Turkish administrators and re-united with Greece. It is estimated that between 1821 and 1912 more than 16,000 people from the area either fled, were killed, or sold into slavery. The newly freed Halkidiki had become under-populated and, in 1922, 29 new villages were established in the area to provide homes for thousands of refugees from Asia Minor.

den Mönchen, die sich auf Athos ansiedelten, Aufzeichnungen geführt. Sie berichten von Aufruhr, Tod und Zerstörungen, die viele Jahre anhielten. Unter den strengen Herrschern, Piraten und Eroberern hatten alle Einheimischen hohe Zollgebühren zu zahlen.

Während des 15. und 16. Jahrhunderts, als die Türken Mazedonien besetzten, flohen viele Griechen nach Chalkidiki, und bedingt durch den Aufschwung der Erzindustrie erlebte die Region in den folgenden zwei Jahrhunderten eine friedliche Zeit. Anfang des 19. Jahrhunderts wurden die Dörfer auf Chalkidiki zu drei Genossenschaften vereinigt, die von einem Stellvertreter der türkischen Regierung verwaltet wurden. Die Bewohner sandten ihre Zollgebühren direkt nach Konstantinopel.

1821 kam es zu einem Aufstand gegen die türkischen Truppen, die die Region beaufsichtigten, als viele Einheimischen sich weigerten, der türkischen Armee beizutreten. Dies führte zu neuen Unruhen, die während der zwei Balkankriege anhielten. Der Friede kehrte 1912 wieder ein, als die griechischen Freiheitskämpfer die Türken von Chalkidiki verjagten und sich wieder mit Griechenland vereinigten. Man schätzt, daß zwischen 1821 und 1912 über 16000 Menschen aus der Region flüchteten, getötet oder als Sklaven verkauft wurden. Das neue, befreite Chalkidiki war jetzt unterbevölkert und 1922 wurden in der Region 29 neue Dörfer gegründet, um Tausenden von Flüchtlingen aus Kleinasien ein neues zu Hause zu gewähren.

Spring landscape in Kassandra
Frühlingslandschaft auf Kassandra

The lively peninsula

Kassandra

Die lebhafte Halbinsel

Sani - Sani Bird Sanctuary / Sani Vogelschutzgebiet -Sani

An easy walk through the woods which skirt the long and beautiful Sani-beach, with views across the wetlands of the Sani Bird Sanctuary (2h. 30m.).

Eine leichte Wanderung durch das Waldgebiet, das unmittelbar im Anschluß an den langen Sani Strand liegt, mit Aussicht auf das Sani Vogelschutzgebiet (2 1/2 Stunden).

The hill of the tower of Stavronikita lies immediately to the west of the Sani-Beach Hotel complex. In the time of the Ancient Greeks there were two cities in the area. Sani, the most important, developed from the prehistoric settlement in the area of the tower. The old city of Sani now lies under the sea.

Der Turm von Stavronikita steht auf dem Kap im Westen des Sani Beach Hotels. In der Antike befanden sich zwei Städte in dieser Region.
Aus einer Ansiedlung, die sich in der Vorgeschichte um den Turm befand, entwickelte sich das antike Sani, eine bedeutende, antike Stadt. Die Ruinen dieser Stadt liegen heute auf dem Meeresgrund.

A bird sanctuary has been created in the wetlands to the east of the woodlands which skirt Sani Beach and a colony of turtles live in a smallpond adjacent to the gates of the agricultural prison; which lies to the east of the wetlands. Tortoises are often seen in the woods.

Das Feuchtgebiet im Anschluß an das Sani Beach Hotel wurde zum Vogelschutzgebiet erklärt und der Teich neben der landwirtschatlichen Strafanstalt ist der Lebensraum für eine Wasserschildkrötenkolonie. Landschildkröten treffen Sie häufig in den Wäldern an.

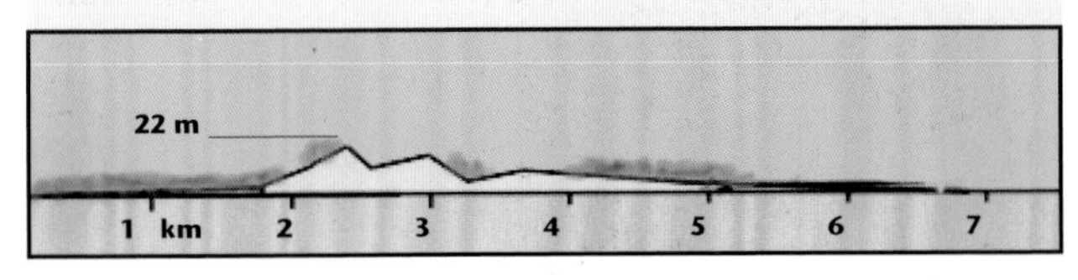

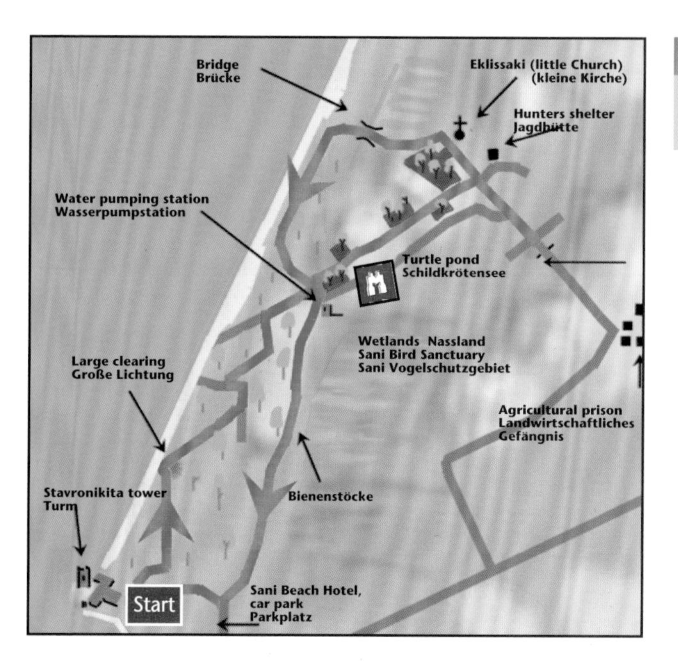

The walk begins at the sandy track immediately to the north of the car park of the Sani Beach Hotel. A sign at the start of the path directs you to Bousoulas Bar. Follow this sandy track to the brow of the slope, then turn right onto the sandy track, which winds in a northeasterly direction through the pinewoods (look for the *'Poseidon'* sign). In about 300m a right hand bend is reached with a wicker basket rubbish bin at its corner. At this point we must leave the main track. Look for the direction sign which indicates the narrow route leading off behind the bin to the southeast. This path soon bears right, then left, passing two large pine trees close together on the left. In a short distance a large cut section of tree trunk is

Die Wanderung beginnt an dem Sandweg, der vom Norden des Sani Beach Hotel Parkplatzes ausgeht. Ein Schild am Anfang des Pfades weist auf die Boussoulas Bar hin. Folgen Sie diesem Pfad bis auf den Hügel, biegen Sie dann rechts auf den Sandweg, der nach Nordosten durch den Kiefernwald führt (schauen Sie nach dem *Poseidon* Zeichen). Nach ungefähr 300m schwenkt die Straße rechts ein. An der Ecke steht ein Abfalleimer. Hier verlassen Sie den Hauptpfad.
Schauen Sie nach dem Wegschild, das den schmalen Pfad Richtung Südosten anzeigt. Der Weg verläuft zuerst rechts, dann links vorbei an zwei eng aneinander liegenden Kiefern. Etwas weiter sehen Sie einen großen, gefällten Baumstamm auf dem Weg Richtung

passed, as the path meanders in a northwesterly direction to reach a large clearing in the woods; lower than the surrounding area. Skirt round the left edge of the clearing and make for the large concrete structure, set into the ground on the far side. The path meanders in a northerly direction for about a kilometre to arrive at the water pumping station, which is used to control the water in the wetlands.

There are many tracks in these woods, so make sure you follow the *'Poseidon'* signs.

This is a good point to stop for a break and look across the wet fields of the Sani bird Sanctuary. However, an even better view will be obtained later in the walk from the olive groves on the slope to the east.

To continue, walk east across the end of the dry water channel near the pumping station towards dense bushes. Bear right before the bushes onto a track, leading briefly north, then east, up a gentle slope, with woodland on the left and an olive grove on the right. the route now takes you over two low hills, passing several small olive groves. Take time to enjoy the expansive view from here of the flooded valley below, before descending to meet the road leading from the coast to the Agricultural Prison, which can be seen on the hill to the west.

Turn left towards the coast, unless you first wish to visit the turtle pond; near the gates of the prison. This involves a detour of 400m

Nordosten liegen. Jetzt kommen Sie auf einer tiefer liegenden Lichtung an. Gehen Sie links um sie herum und auf die Betonkonstruktion weit hinten zu. Der Pfad schlendert nordwärts 1km weiter, bis zu einer Wasserpumpstation. Von hier wird der Wasserstand im ganzen Feuchtgebiet kontrolliert.

Vorsicht, hier gibt es viele Pfade, folgen Sie den Poseidon Schildern. Diese Stelle ist gut geeignet für eine kleine Pause, um einen Blick auf die Umgebung zu werfen. Aber auch etwas später bietet sich von den Olivenhainen am Osthang eine noch bessere Aussicht. Weiter geht es durch den trockengelegten Wasserkanal neben der Pumpstation ostwärts, in Richtung der dichten Büsche. Biegen Sie vor den Büschen rechts auf einen Weg, der zuerst kurz nördlich, dann östlich auf den Hang führt, wo sich zu Ihrer Linken der Wald und zu Ihrer Rechten ein Olivenhain befindet. Es geht über zwei kleine Hügel und an mehreren Olivenhainen vorbei. Nehmen Sie sich Zeit, einen ausgedehnten Blick auf das überflutete Tal zu werfen, bevor Sie wieder absteigen, um auf die Straße vom Strand zur Strafanstalt (vom Hügel aus erkennbar) zu gelangen.

Laufen Sie links auf die Küste zu, es sei denn, Sie wollen zuerst den Schildkrötenteich besichtigen, der sich neben dem Gefängniseingang befindet.

Das bedeutet aber einen Umweg von jeweils 400m hin und zurück. Wenn Sie Richtung Küste weitergehen,

each way. Continuing towards the coast, the track rises gently for 350m then levels out where a track leads off to the right. A brick built hunters' shelter stands a short distance along this track. Our route continues towards the coast. A little further on notice the Eklissaki (little church) in the olive grove to the right of the path. In another 40m the road swings left to skirt the low lying fields and drainage channel between us and the coast. The path wends its way first south and then east until the bridge across the drainage channel is reached. Cross the bridge and take the path to the left, leading onto a hard sandy track, which enters the woods beside the dunes. The sea is very near here and the waves can be clearly heard breaking on the shore. If you prefer to return to Sani along the beach you can do so from this point. If you prefer the shade of the woods, the route continues in a southerly direction for 800m to arrive back at the water pumping station. From here you must decide whether to return via the outward route, via the beach, or via the edge of

steigt de Weg etwa 350m leicht an. Ein Pfad zweigt links ab. Er führt zu einer Jagdhütte. Sie bleiben auf dem Strandweg. Ein Stückchen weiter sehen Sie rechts im Olivenhain ein Eklissaki (kleine Kirche). Nach weiteren 40m schwenkt der Weg nach links und geht um die tiefer gelegenen Felder und den Entwässerungskanal herum. Der Pfad windet sich zuerst südwärts und dann ostwärts bis zur Brücke über dem Entwässerungskanal. Überqueren Sie die Brücke und nehmen Sie den linken Pfad, der auf einen Sandweg in Richtung des Waldes neben den Dünen führt. Sie befinden sich in der Nähe des Meeres und hören die Wellen, die auf den Strand treffen. Wenn Sie wollen, können Sie von diesem Punkt am Strand entlang zum Sani zurückkehren. Wenn Sie aber lieber durch den schattigen Wald wandern wollen, folgen Sie der Route Richtung Süden ca. 800m weit bis zur Pumpstation. Hier müssen Sie sich entscheiden, ob Sie auf der äusseren Route, die Küste entlang oder am Waldrand entlang nach Sani zurückgehen wollen (siehe Landkarte).

Um am Waldrand zurück-

The tower of Stavronikita *Der Turm von Stavronikita*

the wood to Sani (see map). To return via the edge of the wood take the broad farm track which leads south and skirts the woods, passing farm buildings and clusters of beehives along the way. You will encounter beehives like this in woodland all over Halkidiki.* In about 700m the track joins the access road leading from Porto Sani Village to the Sani Beach Hotel. Turn right along this road to arrive at the Sani-Beach Hotel in 400m.

* Beekeeping in Halkidiki
The production of honey is important to the local economy. Many local people keep bees, either as a hobby or an additional source of income. If they are regularly moved, one hive can produce up to 50Kg of pine nectar honey per year. If they are kept in one place only 5kg of honey per year may result.

zukehren, nehmen Sie den breiten Landweg, der südwärts um den Wald führt. Sie kommen an Landhäusern und Bienenstöcken vorbei. Solche Bienenstöcke werden Sie überall in den Wäldern von Chalkidiki antreffen.* Nach 700m trifft der Weg auf die Zufahrtsstraße vom Porto Sani Village zum Sani Beach Hotel. Gehen Sie rechts und nach 400m kommen Sie zum Ausgangspunkt zurück.

*Bienenzucht auf Chalkidiki
Die Herstellung von Honig nimmt einen bedeutenden Anteil der regionalen Wirtschaft ein. Viele Einheimische züchten Bienen, entweder als Hobby oder als zusätzliche Einkommensquelle. Wenn man die Bienenstöcke regelmäßig von einem Gebiet zum anderen bewegt, können sie bis zu 50kg Pinienhonig/pro Bienenstock im Jahr produzieren. Wenn die Bienenstöcke an der gleichen Stelle bleiben, sind es nur ca. 5kg Honig pro Jahr.

Eklissaki

Beehives *Bienenstöcke*

Sani - Sani Camping - Siviri

This walk can be started from either end but the description here is from Porto Sani Village to Siviri. It will be necessary to organise transport for your return, unless you intend to retrace your steps (20km).
The route follows a well marked woodland path which meanders along the cliff tops between Sani Beach Holiday Resort and Siviri, Sani Camping is passed, half way between Sani Beach Holiday Resort and Siviri. People wishing a shorter walk could finish at Sani-Camping.
Because of the nature of the route, care must be taken, particularly with people who may suffer from vertigo, very young children and dogs.

Lizards, birds and butterflies abound in these shady woods, depending on the season. This is one of the most beautiful walks in Halkidiki and should not be missed.

Diese Wanderung kann auf beiden Seiten begonnen werden. Die Wegbeschreibung geht vom Porto Sani Village aus. Sie sollten jedoch für Ihre Rückfahrt vorsorgen, es sei denn, Sie möchten den ganzen Weg wieder zurückwandern (20km).
Die Route folgt einem gut gekennzeichneten Waldpfad, führt über die Klippen zwischen dem Sani Beach Holiday Resort und Siviri, auf halbem Weg vorbei am Sani Camping. Wer eine kürzere Wanderung wünscht, geht nur bis zum Sani Camping. Kleinkinder, Hunde und Personen mit Höhenangst sollten auf dieser Wanderung besonders aufpassen.

Je nach Jahreszeit wimmelt es im schattigen Wald von Echsen, Vögeln und Schmetterlingen. Es handelt sich um eine der schönsten Wanderungen auf Chalkidiki, die sie nicht versäumen sollten!

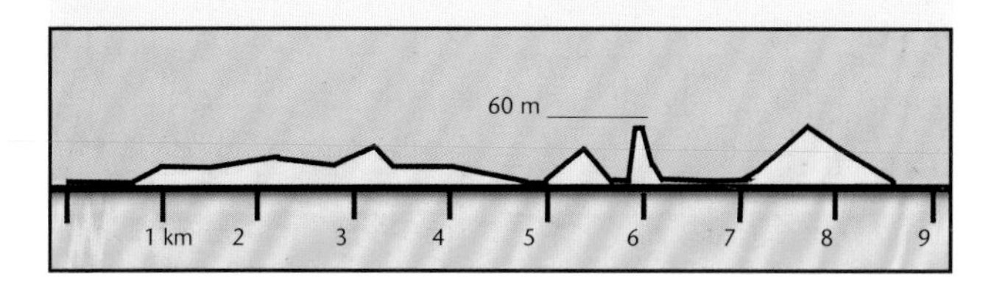

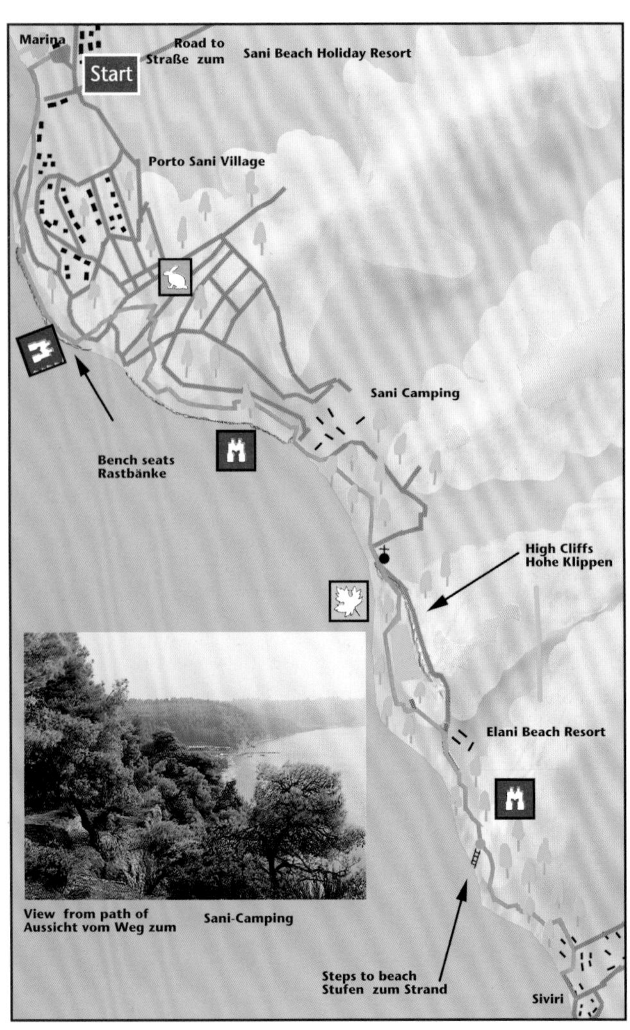

View from path of
Aussicht vom Weg zum
Sani-Camping

This walk can be started from either end but the description here is from Porto Sani Village to Siviri. It will be necessary to organise transport for your return, unless you intend to retrace your steps (20km). The walk starts from the car park of Porto Sani Village, just behind the supermarket. Follow the road leading to the beach, past a taverna on your

Diese Wanderung kann auf beiden Seiten begonnen werden, die Beschreibung geht von Porto Sani Village Richtung Siviri aus. Sie sollten jedoch für Ihre Rückfahrt vorsorgen, es sei denn Sie wandern den ganzen Weg wieder zurück (20km). Folgen Sie vom Parkplatz des Porto Sani Village, hinter dem Supermarkt, der Straße, die

right, where the road turns right towards the marina. Ignore this turn and carry straight on along the path lined with streetlamps until you reach the beach. Turn left and walk along the beach pass sunbed stations, bars and the water sport building until, after 500m or so, stone steps rise to the left. Climb the steps and walk up the road beyond which curves away to the left. Look for the large blue sign across the grass to your right. This indicates a path going into the woods. Follow the Poseidon waymarkers. As you climb with a steep tree covered bank to your left, there are fine views down to the sea on your right. In 450m or so the path broadens to a wider track, which reaches a wide dirt road in a further 200m. Cross the road diagonally to find the continuation of the path. This is the start of a beautiful, easy to follow, path, which meanders through the woods, traverses a gorge and takes us along precipitous headlands. Because of the nature of the route care must be taken, particularly with people, who may suffer from vertigo, very young children and dogs. After 700m of fine walking and dramatic views the path reaches its highest point on a promontory overlooking the sea. Here there are two bench seats to rest your legs. The next part of the journey starts behind the second seat where a path descends gently in a northeasterly to cross a forest road in about 100m. Continue straight on across the road as the path descends through woodland where goats, lizards and butterflies

zum Strand führt. Auf der rechten Seite ist eine Taverne, die Straße geht rechts auf die Marina zu. Sie gehen weiter geradeaus auf dem Weg in Richtung Strand. Dort biegen Sie links ab und laufen den Strand entlang, vorbei an der Strandliegen-Vermietung, den Bars und dem Wassersport-Zentrum. Nach 500m sehen Sie links eine Steintreppe. Steigen Sie hoch und gehen Sie links weiter auf der Straße, die folgt. Ein großes, blaues Schild rechts im Gras deutet auf den Pfad, der in den Wald führt. Achten Sie auf die Poseidon-Zeichen! Steigen Sie links die Böschung hoch und genießen Sie die Aussicht auf das Meer. Nach ca. 450m wird der Pfad breiter und läuft nach weiteren 200m auf eine Straße zu. Überqueren Sie die Straße diagonal und gehen Sie auf dem Pfad weiter. Hier beginnt ein wunderschöner, leichter Weg, der durch den Wald, eine Schlucht und über steile Klippen führt. Kleinkinder, Hunde und Personen mit Höhenangst sollten auf dieser Wanderung besonders aufpassen. Nach 700m erreicht der Weg seinen höchsten Punkt. Ruhen Sie sich auf den zwei Sitzbänken aus und genießen Sie den atemberaubenden Blick aufs Meer. Hinter der zweiten Bank beginnt ein Pfad Richtung Nordosten. Folgen Sie ihm bergab, überqueren Sie nach 100m eine Forststraße und gehen Sie weiter durch den Wald, wo Sie häufig Echsen, Vögel und Schmetterlinge zu sehen bekommen. Mit einer großen Biegung umgehen Sie zu Ihrer

are frequently seen. The reason for the curving descent is apparent when you look down to your right into the massive, forested gorge that the path is circumnavigating. Another forest road is crossed and the descent continues until the neck of the gorge is reached. The foliage here is so dense it forms a complete canopy overhead and the atmosphere is cool and humid. The path now swings round through almost 180 degrees to climb up the other side of the gorge, to cross another forest road in 500m.. The route now turns to the southeast as it continues to climb, to reach the top of the hill. Another road is crossed and the path gently descends to the east. Houses can be seen through the open woodland above and to the left, as the path meanders up and down, for half a kilometre and then drops to a precipitous headland, overlooking the sea. The route now follows the cliffs, descending gradually and giving an occasional glimpse through the trees of the Sani Camping Beach ahead. A small gorge is skirted, a picnic place near the road is passed, and in 350m the beach is reached. Sani Camping, the half way stage of this route, is 200m along the beach. You now have the option to carry on, return the way you came, or book a taxi back to Sani Beach Holiday Resort.

Sani Camping to Siviri

Continue southwards to the end of the beach and take the track, which starts just beyond the Simantro Hotel (look for the Poseidon marker) and follows the clifftop, as it ascends through

The cliff top path near the seats.
Der Klippenweg in der Nähe der Aussichtsbänke

Rechten die tiefe, mit Bäumen bedeckte Schlucht. Nachdem Sie eine weitere Straße überquert haben, kommen Sie zum Anfang der Schlucht. Hier ist das Laub der Bäume so dicht, daß es den Pfad vollkommen überdacht und die Luft ist feucht und kühl. Der Pfad macht eine 180 Grad Schwenke, steigt auf der anderen Seite der Schlucht wieder an, und überquert nach 500m eine Forststraße. Die Route wendet sich Richtung Südosten und erreicht den höchsten Punkt. Überqueren Sie eine weitere Straße und gehen Sie Richtung Osten. Einen halben Kilometer lang geht es auf und ab, und durch das offene Waldgebiet sehen Sie Häuser, bis Sie auf einer steilen Klippe mit Blick auf das Meer angelangt sind. Die Route geht an den Klippen entlang

the trees. This narrow track gradually ascends in a southeasterly direction for about 500m, providing fine views through the trees of the Aegean Sea, with Mt. Olympus (2917m) visible on a clear day. The path now turns to the south as it descends in 300m or so to the beach, where a shallow open valley reaches the sea. A 200m stroll along the beach takes us across the valley and into the woods again, where the path ascends the hillside, keeping close to the clifftops. 200m up the slope the main route leaves the clifftop path to descend the face of the cliff. Look for the Poseidon symbol that marks the descent point. This route takes one down into the previously inaccessible lower plateau of fields and woods and is highly recommended. Those walkers who dislike steep descents can continue on the upper path, which eventually joins

Siviri
The beach below the cliffs
Der Strand unter den Klippen

abwärts und durch die Bäume ist der Sani Camping zu erkennen. Sie umgehen eine kleine Schlucht, kommen an einem Picknickplatz neben der Straße vorbei und erreichen nach 350 m den Strand. Der Sani Camping, das Zwischenziel, liegt in 200m Entfernung vom Strand. Hier haben Sie die Möglichkeit entweder die Wanderung fortzuführen, die gerade gewanderte Strecke zurückzulaufen oder ein Taxi zurück zum Hotel zu bestellen.

Sani Camping nach Siviri: Gehen Sie südwärts bis zum Ende des Strandes und folgen Sie dem Weg, der hinter dem Simandro Hotel beginnt, die Klippen entlang und durch die Bäume führt (schauen Sie nach den Poseidon Zeichen). Dieser Weg steigt etwa 500m Richtung Südosten steil an. Sie sehen die Ägäis und an klaren Tagen den Berg Olymp (2917m). Es geht Richtung Süden, 300m hinunter zum Strand, wo ein flaches, weites Tal bis zum Meer reicht. Gehen Sie 200m am Strand entlang, durch das Tal und wieder in den Wald hinein. Der Pfad steigt wieder die Klippen hoch und nach 200m verläßt er die Hauptroute und führt den Hang hinunter. Schauen Sie nach dem Poseidon Zeichen, das den Abstiegspunkt markiert. Diese Route ist sehr zu empfehlen, denn sie führt abwärts zu den schwer zugäglichen Feldern. Wenn Sie keine steilen Abstiege mögen, gehen Sie auf dem oberen Pfad weiter, bis Sie auf die Waldstraße stoßen. Die beiden Routen vereinigen sich wieder beim

the forest road. The two routes re-combine above Elani Beach Resort, a holiday centre (see the map).
Descend the cliff face using the steps provided. The path meanders down through virgin forest, giving occasional sea views through the trees, as it twists and turns its way southwards to emerge in a cornfield after 500m. Follow the farm track round the seaward edge of the field and into the wood, where it runs parallel to the beach on the right and the cornfield on the left. In 500m the end of the cornfield is reached and the track continues through the forest for a further 200m to arrive at a grassy woodland track, leading to the beach. Turn left onto this track which leads eastwards for 100m and then becomes a dirt road as it climbs the hill to arrive at a track junction in a further 100m. This is the point where the upper alternative route, mentioned earlier, meets the lower route. Turn right onto this track to descend, in 400m, to Elani Beach Resort. At the southern end of the beach is a wall, shaded by trees, ideal for a short rest.
From Elani Beach Resort the route leads southwards, back into the woods, and meanders through the woods, following the coast to arrive, in 700m at an open grassy area on the clifftop. Fine views of the coast can be seen from this vantagepoint. In addition there is a stairway down the cliff giving access to the beach, for those who wish to rest a while, or go for a swim. The path now continues southwards, initially skirting, then re-entering the woodland. The path meanders up and down,

Elani Beach Resort (siehe Karte).
Steigen Sie auf der Treppe die Böschung hinunter. Der Pfad führt durch unberührte Natur und bietet durch die Bäume Blick aufs Meer, bis er nach 500m südwärts auf ein Kornfeld stößt. Folgen Sie dem Feldweg, der von der Meerseite das Feld umgeht und in den Wald hineinführt, indem Sie parallel zum Strand und zum Feld laufen. Nach 500m ist das Feld zu Ende und der Weg geht weiter durch den Wald. Nach 200m gelangen Sie auf einen grasbedeckten Waldweg, der zum Strand führt. Biegen Sie links in diesen Weg ein und nach 100m Richtung Osten wechselt er zu einer Straße über, die nach weiteren, ansteigenden 100m an eine Weggabelung anlangt. Hier treffen die beiden vorhin erwähnten Routen aufeinander. Steigen Sie auf dem rechten Weg 400m ab zum Elani Beach Resort. Am Ende des Strandes neben einer Mauer finden Sie ein schattiges Plätzchen zum Rasten.
Von hier verläuft die Route weiter südwärts zurück in den Wald, am Hang entlang, bis Sie nach 700m auf einer Wiese auf der Höhe der Klippen ankommen. Von diesem Aussichtspunkt haben Sie schöne Aussicht auf das Meer. Einige Stufen führen hinunter zum Strand. Wer möchte, kann eine kleine Pause machen oder schwimmen gehen. Der Weg führt dann in den Wald zurück. Durch den Wald führt der Weg in leichtem Auf und Ab. Es gibt hier viele Wege, deshalb achten Sie bitte auf die Schilder, damit Sie keinen

changing direction frequently as it traverses the contours of this beautiful woodland. There are many tracks so follow the markers to ensure you keep to the correct route. After 500m or so the woodland is dotted with clumps of 'Prickly Pear' cactus as the outskirts of Siviri are approached. The track now leaves the woods to join an adjacent dirt road, which takes us the remaining 200m or so into the village. Make for the seafront to take you past holiday accommodation and a Taverna, where you can slake your thirst. A taxi can be ordered from here back to Sani Beach Holiday Resort if required.

falschen Weg einschlagen! Nach ca. 500m sehen Sie eine Lichtung, bewachsen mit Kaktusfeigen und in der Ferne ist bereits Siviri zu erkennen. Der Pfad verbindet sich jetzt mit einem Feldweg und führt die letzten 200m ins Dorf. Gehen Sie Richtung Meer an den Ferienwohnungen vorbei und zu einer der Tavernen. Hier können Sie Ihren Durst löschen oder wenn nötig, ein Taxi für die Rückfahrt bestellen.

A group of walkers enjoying a taverna meal after walking from Sani to Siviri in late October

Eine Wandergruppe beim Essen in einer Taverne. Es ist Oktober und sie haben gerade eine Wanderung von Sani nach Siviri zurückgelegt.

Possidi - Pinewoods / Kiefernwälder - Possidi

An easy, circular, ridge walk in the pinewoods above the Possidi beach which provides beautiful views of the coast as well as the olive grove covered valley inland, towards Kalandra. The route follows forest tracks for most of the way.
Time:- 2 hours

The start and finish of the walk is from the coast road 300m south of the Possidi Holidays Hotel. There is ample parking on open ground just past the hotel, if the road at the start is too busy to park there.

14th century documents in Mt. Athos mention Possidi, but as the name relates to the worship of *Poseidon*, the god of the sea, it was probably named in much earlier times.

Eine leichte Rundwanderung über Felder und durch Pinienwälder auf dem Höhenrücken oberhalb des Possidi Strandes und durch das breite, mit Olivenhainen bestandene Tal, das zum Ort Kalandra führt. Die Route führt größtenteils über Ziegenpfade und bietet hervorragende Aussicht auf die Küste.
Dauer: 2 Stunden
Ausgangspunkt und Endziel dieser Route ist die Verbindungsstraße zum Possidi Holidays Hotel, ca. 300 Meter südlich des Hotels.

Possidi wird schon im 14. Jahrhundert in den schriftlichen Aufzeichnungen auf Athos erwähnt. Da der Name mit der Verehrung des Meeresgottes *Poseidon* zusammenhängt, hat er wahrscheinlich einen viel älteren Ursprung.

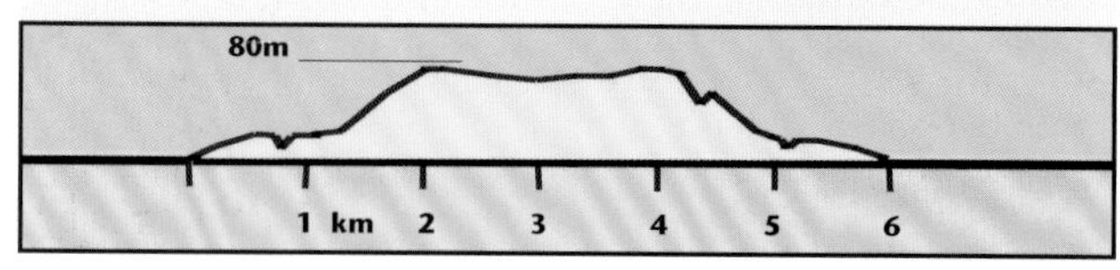

Follow the tarmac road that leads away from the beach and towards the woods. In 120m the tarmac ends and the unsurfaced road turns to the left. Ignore this turn and

Folgen Sie der asphaltierten Straße, die vom Strand in Richtung Wald führt. Nach 120m ist die Straße nicht mehr geteert und führt nach links. Achten Sie nicht auf

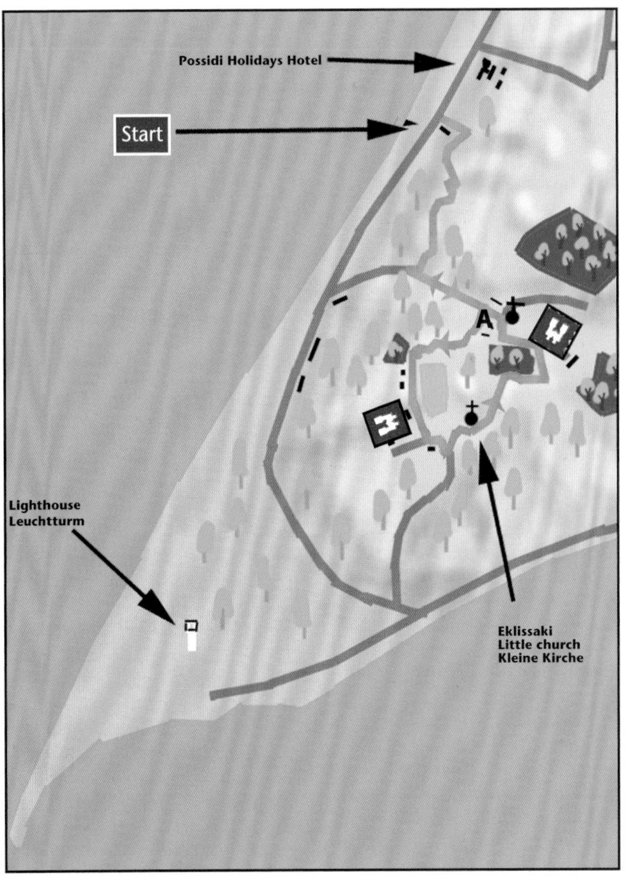

carry straight on into the woods on a sandy track. After another 120m the sandy track swings round to the west, to climb the hillside, giving sea views to the right as it crests the rise and turns to the south. The route now passes through open woodland to reach a shallow ravine in another 200m. Follow the low earth wall of the ravine round to the point where steps are cut in the bank. The path now crosses the ravine, avoiding wet patches by contouring round through the tall rushes, to climb back

diese Abzweigung, sondern gehen Sie weiter geradeaus auf einem Feldweg in den Wald hinein. Nach weiteren 120 Metern steigt der Weg Richtung Westen auf einen Hügel. Hier haben Sie zu Ihrer rechten Seite einen herrlichen Blick auf das Meer. Jetzt gehen Sie Richtung Süden, durch den Wald und nach 200m kommen Sie in ein kleines Tal. Folgen Sie dem kleinen Erdwall, bis zu einer Stelle, wo Treppenstufen zu sehen sind. Hier überqueren Sie das kleine Tal, ohne in die feuchten Stellen zu treten, am

up into the wood at the other side. Look for the waymarkers. Continue on in a south westerly direction, following the waymarkers on the trees, to arrive in 200m or so on a small ridge. Here we turn left, decending slightly, as the route passes through some dense bush to arrive, in 120m, at more open ground (an old olive grove). In another 130m of walking a farm access road is reached, with a ploughed field beyond containing olive trees.

Turn left and follow the farm track to the top of the hill to arrive at several turreted apartment buildings on a track junction (point A on the map). Turn right here as the route now climbs up into the pinewoods, turning to the west as it does so. Notice the polythene bags attached to the pine trees, which are collecting pine resin, used in the production of 'Retsina,'the popular, local wine.* In fine weather there are beautiful coastal views to the right as the track climbs through the forest along the ridge to reach a height of 70m above the sea. Eventually the track starts to descend, turning southwards once more with an olive grove to the right and open fields to the left. Ahead and far below can be seen the spit of sand which reaches out into the sea, marking the Cap (Akrotiri) of Possidi. The path continues to descend to the south, passing to the left of several properties, to reach a junction on an open headland. Turn left and follow the track down and round to a second junction on a bend. The road to the right leads down to the sea. We must turn left to

besten indem Sie sich an den hohen Binsen richten. Auf der anderen Seite angekommen geht es wieder hinauf in den Wald. Schauen Sie nach den Wegmarkierungen. Folgen Sie den Markierungen an den Bäumen in Richtung Südwesten, bis Sie nach ca. 200m auf dem Hügel angelangt sind. Hier biegen Sie links ab. Es geht wieder abwärts durch die dichten Büsche, bis Sie nach 120m auf ein offenes Feld kommen (ein alter Olivenhain). Nach 130m erreichen Sie eine Zufahrtsstraße zu einem Bauernhof. Dahinter liegt ein gerodetes Feld mit Olivenbäumen.

Biegen Sie nach links und folgen Sie der Zufahrtsstraße bis auf den Hügel, wo sich einige Ferienappartments an einer Kreuzung befinden (Punkt A auf der Karte). Biegen Sie rechts ab. Der Weg führt Richtung Westen bergauf in den Kiefernwald hinein. Beachten Sie die Plastiktüten, die an den Kiefern hängen. Darin wird das Pinienharz aufgefangen, das für die Herstellung des bekannten, ortstypischen *Retsina-Weins** gebraucht wird. Wenn Sie nach rechts schauen, können Sie bei klarem Wetter eine wunderschöne Aussicht auf die Küste genießen. Unsere Wanderung führt weiter durch den Wald, auf ca. 70m Höhe ü.M.

Schließlich geht es wieder bergab Richtung Süden. Der Weg schlängelt sich durch weite Felder zu der linken und einem Olivenhain zu der rechten Seite. Weit hinten in der Ferne ist das, weit in das Meer reichende Kap von

continue along the ridge, walking north then east on a track which first descends and then climbs up through the forest, as it circles round the deep gorge to the right. After 300m or so the track bears sharp left (Note the small Eklissaki at the corner) and continues level at first and then climbs past beehives as it curves first to the southeast, then to the north, to reach its highest point before turning west on the return route. From here the broad valley between the coast and Kalandra lies to our right, and as the path turns west again a fine view is obtained over this open expanse with its rows of olive trees interspersed with woodland and the occasional building. The path now descends, with an olive grove on the left, to reach a junction on a steep descent, where there is another Eklissaki on the corner. Our route follows the track leading westwards back up the hill to arrive at point A on the map, once more (near the turreted apartment blocks). From here retrace your steps back to the Possidi Holidays Hotel.

* Retsina has been produced in Greece since ancient times. The pine resin, originally added as a natural preservative, gives the wine its distinctive flavour. In earlier days it was collected by cutting away a strip of bark on a pine tree and fastening a tin container to the tree to collect the sap that oozed out as the tree repaired the wound. When the sap stopped running a further strip of bark was removed below the first and so on. Nowadays the pinesap or

Possidi (Akrotiri) zu erkennen. Der Weg führt weiter Richtung Süden abwärts, vorbei an einigen Grundstücken und kommt zu einer Gabelung mitten in der Landschaft. Biegen Sie links ab und folgen Sie dem Pfad hinunter zu einer zweiten Gabelung in einer Kurve. Die rechte Straße führt direkt zum Meer. Sie gehen links weiter, dem Höhenrücken entlang, zuerst in nördliche und dann in östliche Richtung und folgen diesem Weg, der erst etwas abwärts führt und dann wieder aufwärts, durch den Wald und um eine tiefe Schlucht herum auf der rechten Seite. Nach 300m biegt der Weg scharf links ab (achten Sie auf das kleine Eklissaki in der Ecke), er ist anfangs noch flach und steigt dann wieder an. Vorbei an Bienenstöcken wandern Sie nach Südosten und dann nach Norden, um am höchsten Punkt anzukommen. Jetzt wandern wir Richtung Westen zurück. Zu Ihrer Rechten liegt das breite Tal zwischen der Küste und Kalandra, und während der Weg weiter westwärts führt, bieten sich schöne Ausblicke über das Innere der Kassandra. Sie durchqueren einige Olivenhaine, dazwischen ab und zu kurze Waldstücke. Links und rechts finden sich selten einige Gebäude.

Der Weg geht abwärts, links an einem Olivenhain vorbei, zu einer Kreuzung an einem steilen Abhang. In der Ecke steht noch ein Eklissaki. Die Route folgt dem Richtung Westen einschlagenden Pfad zurück auf den Hügel, wo Sie zu dem Punkt A auf der Karte zurückkehren (in der Nähe

resin is collected in heavy-duty polythene bags and these are often to be seen fastened to trees in the pine forest.

Collecting resin from the pinetrees

Das Harzaufsammeln von den Kiefern

der Ferienappartments).
Von hier folgen Sie dem bekannten Weg zurück zum Possidi Holidays Hotel.

* Der Retsina-Wein wurde in Griechenland schon in der Antike hergestellt. Das Kiefernharz, ursprünglich als natürliches Konservierungsmittel zugefügt, gibt dem Wein diesen unverkennbaren Geschmack. Früher wurde es aufgesammelt, indem man eine Baumrinde aufschnitt und einen Metallbehälter an die Kiefer band. Aus der Rinde tropfte ein Saft, mit dem der Baum seine Wunde schloß, direkt in den Behälter. Wenn kein Saft mehr herauslief, wurde ein neuer Streifen aus der Rinde entfernt. Heutzutage wird der Kiefernsaft oder das Harz in strapazierfähigen Plastiktüten aufgefangen. Man sieht sie häufig an den Bäumen in den Kiefernwäldern.

Cap Possidi

Polychrono - Turtles Schildkröten-teich - Polychrono

This walk takes one up into the hills behind Polychrono to visit a pond in the woods where turtles are found. The route follows broad forest tracks, passing through a high valley, surrounded by sandstone cliffs and pine forest. The return path, gives many fine views of the sea and coast as it gradually descends, through the trees, to Polychrono.

These pine woods contain many large trees, often reaching up towards the light from the bottoms of deep gorges, which are covered with dense undergrowth. This provides a fine habitat for birds, small mammals and insects. Tortoises and lizards are often encountered as well as the turtles.

Depending on the season, the more open ground can be a mass of colour, with its flowers, shrubs and butterflies.

Diese Wanderung führt in die Berge hinter Polychrono, wo sich im Wald versteckt ein Teich mit Wasserschildkröten befindet. Die Route verläuft auf breiten Waldwegen und durch ein hochgelegenes Tal, umgeben von sandigen Klippen und Pinienwäldern. Auf dem Rückweg steigen Sie geradewegs durch den Wald nach Polychrono ab, während schöne Blicke auf das Meer und die Küste Sie begleiten.

In den Pinienwäldern stehen sehr hohe Bäume, die aus dem Grund tiefer mit dichtem Unterholz bedeckter Schluchten herauswachsen. Ein idealer Lebensraum für Vögel, kleine Säugetiere und Insekten.
Auch Landschildkröten und Eidechsen, sowie Wasserschildkröten sind hier anzutreffen. Das offene Land bietet je nach Jahreszeit ein farbenprächtiges Bild, mit Blumen, Büschen und Schmetterlingen.

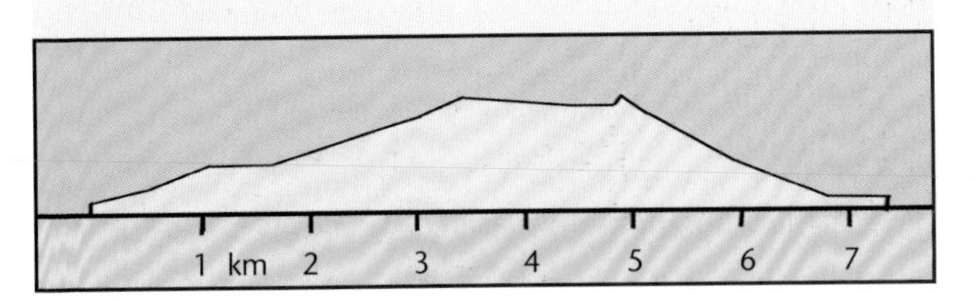

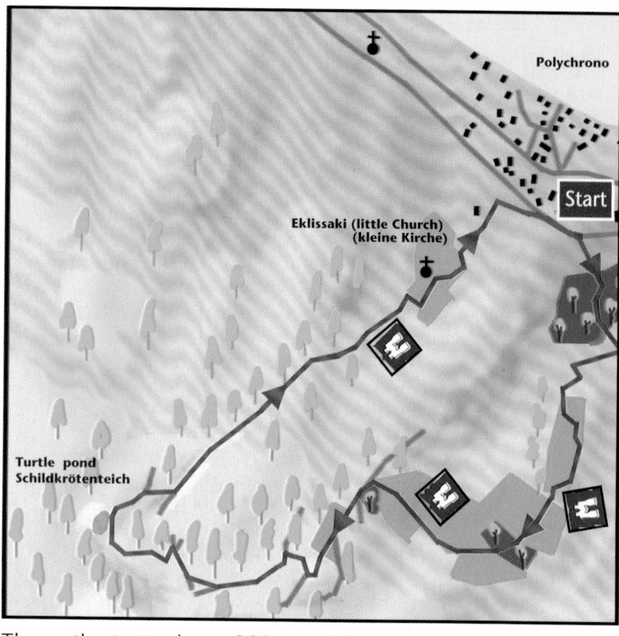

The path starts about 300m past the traffic lights in Polychrono, just opposite a small supermarket. Here a track leads southeast towards the hills behind the village. Ignore the large blue notice near the traffic lights, that indicates another route to the turtles. Our route is quieter, more scenic and you are less likely to be bothered by traffic. The sandy track, rising from the village, passes through pine trees to arrive at an olive grove in 300m. The path continues in a southerly direction to arrive at a junction. Turn right here to follow the track, that leads first southwest, then south-east, then southwest again to arrive at a cornfield. The track enters the field, first keeping to the right side and then crossing the field to follow the left edge for a total distance of about 400m. The route

Die Wanderung beginnt 300m von der Verkehrsampel in Polychrono entfernt, gegenüber eines kleinen Supermarktes. Ein Pfad führt Richtung Südosten, in die Berge hinter dem Dorf. Ignorieren Sie das große, blaue Schild in der Nähe der Ampel, das auf eine andere Route zum Schildkrötenteich hinweist. Die hier beschriebene Route ist viel ruhiger, malerischer und vor allem verkehrsfrei. Auf dem Feld-weg, der vom Dorf ausgeht, kommen Sie nach 300m durch die Pinienbäume an einem Olivenhain an. Der Weg geht weiter südwärts bis zu einer Gabelung. Biegen Sie rechts in einen Weg ein, der zuerst Richtung Südwesten, dann Südosten, und wieder Südwesten einschlägt und an einem Weizenfeld anlangt. Zuerst gehen Sie auf der rechten Seite des Feldes

then swings west across the field towards a small patch of woodland. On each of these westerly traverses fine views of the coast can be observed to the right. The path briefly enters the woods and then emerges into another corn-field situated in open terrain, which provides fine views to the north and east. The route takes us across the middle of this field and then into a grove of young olive trees. At the end of the olives turn right and follow the track due west across more fields. Eventually about 800m after leaving the woodland the path arrives at a junction, with a young olive grove on the corner. Turn left here, following the route south for 50m, to the next fork. Take the right hand branch of the fork, which continues south, for 250m to arrive at another fork. Turn right again, keeping to the higher track, which eventually levels out and provides a fine view across the valley to the left. At the next junction again keep right as the track climbs to the north through the woods and then turns east to another junction. Here our route joins up with the main track through these woods and the junction is clearly marked with turtle and drinking water signs, which indicate that we should turn left up the hill. We now ascend to the southwest through mature forest along a broad forest track, which may have beehives lining the route. After 350m a junction is reached at a high point. Once more the now familiar signs mark the way and we turn right, gradually descending to the north. In a

entlang, danach überqueren Sie das Feld und gehen ca. 400m auf der linken Seite weiter. Dann führt die Route nach Westen ab, zu einer kleinen Waldfläche. Dabei haben Sie zu Ihrer Rechten schöne Aussicht auf die Küste. Der Weg führt nur ein kurzes Stück durch den Wald und mündet dann in ein anderes Weizenfeld. Von hier bietet sich schöne Aussicht nach Norden und Osten. Der Weg geht bis zu der Mitte des Feldes und biegt dann in einen Olivenhain mit jungen Bäumen ein. Am Ende des Haines biegen Sie nach rechts und gehen auf dem Weg weiter, Richtung Westen, wo sich weitere Weizenfelder befinden. Nachdem Sie sich ungefähr 800m von dem Waldgebiet entfernt haben, kommen Sie an eine Gabelung, in deren Ecke ein Olivenbaumhain steht. Biegen Sie nach links, gehen Sie 50m nach Süden bis zu einer zweiten Gabelung, biegen Sie wieder rechts und gehen Sie Richtung Süden weiter bis nach 250m erneut eine Kreuzung erscheint. Biegen Sie wieder rechts auf den höheren Pfad, der langsam ansteigt und zu Ihrer Linken einen herrlichen Blick auf das darunterliegende Tal erlaubt. An der nächsten Gabelung halten Sie sich wieder rechts und wandern Richtung Norden durch den Wald bis zu einer neuen Kreuzung. Hier verbindet sich die Route mit der Hauptroute. Auf der Kreuzung befinden sich Hinweisschilder mit den Aufschriften: *Schildkröten* und *Trinkwasser*, die nach links den Berg hinaufweisen. Jetzt steigen Sie auf einem breiten

further 250m the track splits three ways. Turn sharp left here as the route first descends to the south and then turns west again, gradually descending towards the floor of the deep, tree filled gorge to the right. To the left are high sandstone cliffs and to the right very large pine trees, many covered with dense ivy. In a short distance the track drops steeply as it curves right to reach the valley floor adjacent to the turtle pond. Here there are picnic tables, a drinking water fountain, and seats from which to view the turtles.

To return to Polychrono continue past the pond on the same forest track to reach a junction in a short distance. Turn right here and follow the road as it gradually descends to the east for about 200m. As the track begins to descend more steeply to the north, look for a Poseidon sign. This indicates the start of a narrow path going east away from the track. Follow this path for 100m to arrive at a steep earth bank. A graded path leads up this bank to emerge onto a broad but

Weg durch den Wald auf. Am Wegrand stehen häufig schön hintereinander gereihte Bienenstöcke. Nach 350m kommen Sie oben an einer Kreuzung an. Auch hier sind Wegweiser angebracht, die nach rechts zeigen, und es geht geradewegs abwärts Richtung Norden. Nach weiteren 250m teilt sich der Weg in drei Pfade auf. Gehen Sie scharf links. Der Pfad biegt zuerst südlich ab und führt dann wieder nach Westen, geradewegs auf den Grund der tiefen, dichtbewachsenen Schlucht zu. Auf der linken Seite befinden sich Sandsteinklippen und auf der rechten sehr hohe Pinienbäume, die mit dichtem Efeu bedeckt sind. Nach kurzer Zeit fällt der Pfad steil nach rechts ins Tal, das am Schildkrötenteich angrenzt. Hier gibt es Picknicktische, einen Trinkwasserbrunnen und Sitzbänke, von denen man die Wasserschildkröten beobachten kann.

Der Rückweg folgt dem Weg, der am Teich vorbei bis zu einer Gabelung etwas südöstlich führt. Biegen Sie hier rechts ab und folgen Sie ca. 200m der Straße Richtung Osten. Wenn dieser etwas steiler wird und Richtung Norden geht, müßten Sie einen Poseidon-Wegweiser erblicken. Von hier folgen Sie einem schmalen Pfad Richtung Westen. Gehen Sie 100m bis zu einem steilen Erdwall. Treppenstufen führen über diese Böschung zu einem breiten, aber relativ unbenutzten Waldweg. Der Rest der Strecke geht auf diesem Weg durch die Wälder und die Felder zurück nach Polychrono. Während Sie die

relatively unused forest track above. The rest of the walk follows this track as it descends through fine woodland and farmland, to Polychrono. As you walk the 3km back down to the village you will pass a beautiful little white church on the edge of a cornfield, and a little further on, a goat shelter. You can also enjoy the panoramic view ahead of the coastline, the gulf and the hills of Sithonia beyond. On a clear day Mt. Athos is easily seen. The path finally emerges onto the main street of Polychrono near the traffic lights.

3km zurück ins Dorf absteigen, kommen Sie an einer wunderschönen, kleinen, weißen Kapelle am Rande eines Weizenfeldes, und etwas weiter an einem Ziegenpferch vorbei.
Genießen Sie den Panoramablick auf die Küstenlinie, das Meer und die Berge von Sithonia im Hintergrund. An klaren Tagen ist sogar der Berg Athos zu erkennen. Schließlich kommen Sie wieder auf der Hauptstraße von Polychrono, in der Nähe der Verkehrsampel an.

A little church on the Polychrono walk (January 2000)
Eine kleine Kirche auf der Polychrono Wanderung (Januar 2000)

Goats of Halkidiki *Ziegen auf Chalkidiki*

Kriopigi - Kassandrino - Kriopigi

This walk, which is quite long, takes one via forest tracks to the beautiful little village of Kassandrino, hidden away in the hills of Kassandra. This unspoilt Greek village is a delight to visit. The return route to Kriopigi also uses forest tracks that take one through the more remote parts of this peninsula.

Diese Wanderung ist relativ lang und führt auf Waldwegen zum wunderschönen, kleinen Dorf Kassandrino, das versteckt in den Bergen von Kassandra liegt. Es wird Ihnen großes Vergnügen bereiten, dieses noch unberührte, griechische Dorf zu entdecken. Der Rückweg erfolgt auch auf Feldwegen, durch die kaum erschlossene Region der Halbinsel.

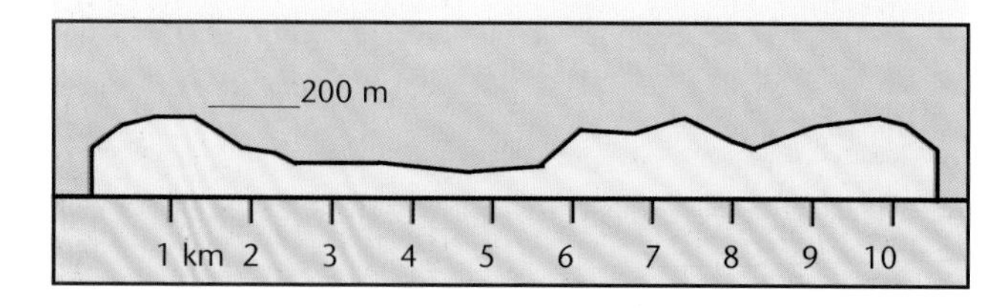

The walk begins beside the church in Kriopigi. On entering the village from the north turn right into the old village immediately after passing under the second set of flashing amber traffic signals.
From the church take the concrete road that leads southwest, up towards the woods. This zig zags up the hill, past houses, eventually becoming an unmade access road. From here, looking back there is a good view of the sea across to Turtle Island and Sithonia beyond. In 300m a junction is reached.
The road to the right leads up to Ag. Paraskevi (Holy Friday),

Ausgangspunkt ist die Kirche in Kriopigi. Wenn Sie vom Norden in das Dorf kommen, biegen Sie rechts in das alte Dorf ein, direkt nach der zweiten Ampel.
Von der Kirche gehen Sie auf der betonierten Straße südwestwärts, hinauf in den Wald. Es geht im Zickzack aufwärts, vorbei an einigen Häusern, bis die Straße in einen Feldweg übergeht. Von hier haben Sie schöne Aussicht zurück auf das Meer, auf die Schildkröteninsel und Sithonia dahinter. Nach 300m erreichen Sie eine Kreuzung. Die rechte Straße führt nach Agia Paraskevi (der Heilige Freitag), und von dort

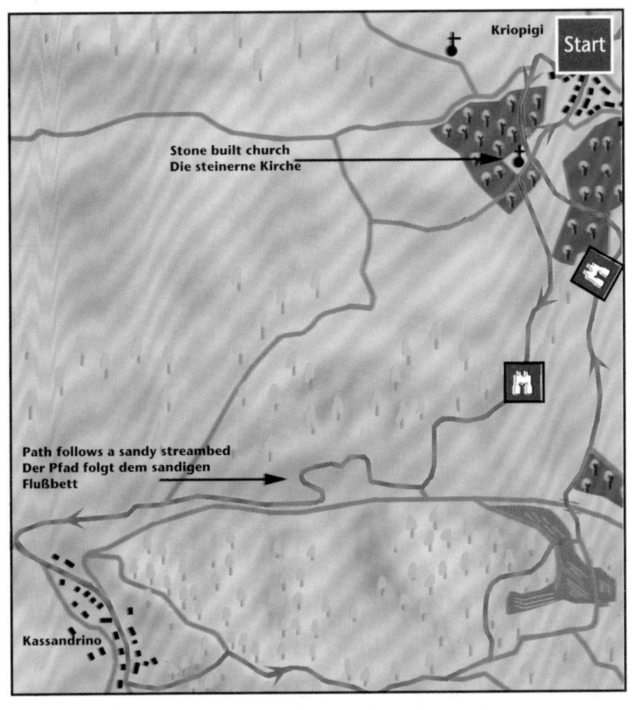

about 500m away, and thence to Kassandria, where there is an excellent market on a Tuesday. A possible extra walk for a Tuesday would be to visit the chapel of Ag. Paraskevi and then carry on to Kassandria (about two and a half hours) for the market, returning by bus or taxi to Kriopigi.

To continue to Kassandrino ignore this right turn to pass through olive groves and arrive at a goat drinking trough in 250m. Only 100m further on a junction is reached, signed *Kassandrino* to the right. Turn right here, heading south up the hill, past a fine stone built church. About 200 m further on a track leads off to the left. Leave the main track here and follow this minor track across

nach Kassandria, wo es dienstags immer einen schönen Markt gibt. Eine gute Möglichkeit für eine Wanderung wäre also, an einem Dienstag die Kirche Agia Paraskevi zu besichtigen, dann weiter nach Kassandria zum Markt zu wandern (ca. 2,5 Stunden) und von dort mit dem Bus oder Taxi zurück nach Kriopigi zu fahren.

Um nach Kassandrino zu kommen, meiden Sie diese rechte Abzweigung und gehen weiter geradeaus durch Olivenhaine, bis Sie nach 250m an einen Wassertrog für Ziegen kommen. Nur 100m weiter erreichen Sie eine Kreuzung, wo ein Wegweiser mit der Aufschrift *Kassandrino* nach rechts zeigt. Biegen Sie rechts ab und gehen Sie den Berg

the field and down the slope beyond. The track descends quickly at first, as it curves round to the west, with steep woodland on the right. In about 2km the track turns away from the wood and travels due south across fields, to eventually arrive at an asphalt road. Before reaching the road the track arrives at a dry sandy stream bed, which is bone dry for most of the year. Turn right onto this stream bed and follow it all of the way to Kassandrino, a distance of about 4 km along the valley bottom. At the village turn left, up onto the road, just before the bridge. It is only 500 m along the road to the village centre, where there are two fine traditional tavernas.

Having refreshed oneself in this delightful place, continue on down the main street towards the end of the village. Here an obvious narrow path can be seen winding up a low ridge to the left, above the houses, and entering the trees. Look for the Poseidon waymarker signs that indicate the start of this track which takes one between houses, with tractors and farm implements parked, up onto the hillside. In a short distance the narrow path widens into a forest road which leads quite steeply upwards to arrive at the main forest road that follows the ridge above the village. Turn right onto the main track and follow it all of the way, as it meanders eastward, for two kilometres, gradually gaining height. This ridge route passes through fine open woodland with steep valleys falling away on both sides and occasional cultivated

hinauf, vorbei an einer sehr schönen, aus Stein gebauten Kirche. 200m weiter zweigt ein Pfad nach rechts ab. Hier verlassen Sie die Hauptstraße und folgen diesem Abzweig über ein Feld den Hang hinunter. Der Pfad geht schnell bergab und dreht dann nach Westen, mit den steilen Waldhängen zu Ihrer Rechten. Nach 2km entfernen Sie sich vom Waldgebiet und der Pfad führt Sie Richtung Süden, über die Felder, bis Sie schließlich eine Asphaltstraße erreichen. Bevor Sie die Straße erreichen, kommen Sie an einem sandigen Flußbett an, das meist trocken ist. Biegen Sie rechts in dieses Flußbett ein und folgen Sie ihm bis nach Kassandrino - eine Strecke von ungefähr 4 km immer den Talgrund entlang. Kurz vor der Brücke am Rand des Dorfes biegen Sie nach links, auf die Straße. Von hier sind es nur noch 500m bis zur Dorfmitte, wo es zwei schöne, traditionelle Tavernen gibt.

Nachdem Sie eine Erfrischungspause eingelegt haben, gehen Sie auf der Hauptstraße bis zum Ende des Dorfes. Deutlich erkennen Sie hier einen schmalen Pfad, der links die Bergflanke hinaufführt, vorbei an den Häusern, und hin zu den Bäumen. Schauen Sie nach dem Poseidon - Wegweiser, der den Start dieser Strecke andeutet. Es geht vorbei an Bauernhöfen mit Traktoren und Pflügen, aufwärts in Richtung der Hügelkette. Nach kurzer Zeit weitet sich der Pfad zu einer Forststraße aus, die ziemlich steil bergauf führt und auf die Forststraße führt, die den Gebirgsrücken über dem Dorf folgt. Biegen

fields, where the ridge widens slightly. Keep to the main track and look for the waymarker signs, whenever a fork is reached. After 2km of walking, and just after a slight curving descent to the left, the track curves gently right and climbs again, as a field is passed on the right. Look for the waymarker on a tree to the left here, just before the brow of the hill. This indicates the start of a steep descent to the left, through the wood, following an old resin collectors' path. Follow the waymarkers through the wood as the path descends to the north and then turns east through delightful woodland. A field will be seen on the right, through the trees. In 1 km the path emerges onto a track with a field directly opposite. Cross at the bottom of the field and follow the markers through the hedge to a track. Turn left onto the track to arrives at the asphalt road between Kassindrino and Kriopigi in a short distance. Turn right onto the road for only 25m, then cross the road and turn left onto another track This track

Spring in Halkidiki
Frühling in Chalkidiki

Sie rechts auf diese Straße und folgen Sie ihr immer bergauf, über 2km Richtung Osten. Diese Wanderroute führt durch weite, offene Waldgebiete, mit steil nach unten abfallenden Schluchten zu beiden Seiten der Strecke, und Wiesen, überall wo der Bergkamm flacher ist. Bleiben Sie auf der Forststraße und schauen Sie jedesmal nach den Wegweisern, wo immer Sie eine Gabelung antreffen. Nach 2km sehen Sie eine Linkskurve, die abwärts führt, Sie bleiben auf dem Weg, der leicht nach rechts und wieder hinauf an einem Feld vorbei führt. Kurz vor der Bergkuppe schauen Sie auf der linken Seite nach einem Wegweiser an einem Baum. Hier beginnt ein steiler Abstieg durch den Wald, auf einem Weg, der früher von den Harzsammlern benutzt wurde. Folgen Sie den Wegweisern, die Sie im Wald antreffen. Der Weg geht zuerst nordwärts und dann ostwärts duch eine wunderschöne Waldlandschaft.

Durch die Bäume können Sie ein Feld auf der rechten Seite sehen. Nach 1 km mündet der Weg in einen Pfad ein, direkt gegenüber liegt ein Feld. Gehen Sie am Rande des Feldes entlang und folgen Sie den Wegweisern durch die Hecke auf einen Pfad. Biegen Sie rechts ab, gehen Sie nur 25m geradeaus, bis ein anderer Pfad den Weg kreuzt. Biegen Sie links ab und steigen Sie auf diesem Pfad Richtung Norden 300m durch einen Olivenhain ab, bis zu einer Gabelung. Gehen Sie links weiter Richtung Norden und hinauf auf den Hauptweg, der nach Kriopigi führt. Schließlich kommen Sie nach 600m auf die Bergspitze,

travels northward, climbing slightly through an olive grove to arrive at a junction in 300m. Turn left here and continue northwards, keeping to the main track all of the way as it climbs up the hill towards Kriopigi. Eventually, after 600m or so the top is reached with sea views, through the olive grove, to the right. The path now descends through olive groves, and smallholdings to arrive back, in another 600m, at the junction near the stone church, mentioned earlier. The circuit is complete. It now only remains to retrace your steps back to the village to seek out a Taverna.

von der Sie über den Olivenhain zu Ihrer Rechten bis aufs Meer sehen können. Der Pfad geht jetzt weitere 600m bergab durch Olivenhaine und kleinere abgetrennte Grundstücke, bis zu der Kreuzung in der Nähe der steinernen Kirche, die Sie schon auf dem Hinweg angetroffen haben. Hier ist die Rundwanderung abgeschlossen. Sie brauchen nur noch auf dem gleichen Weg zurück ins Dorf zu wandern und eine Taverne aufzusuchen.

Hanioti

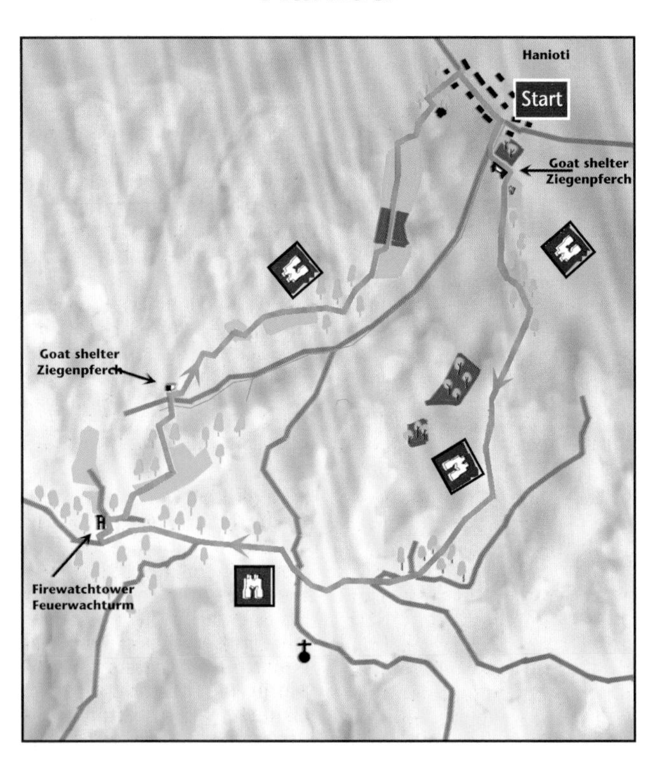

Hanioti - Fire Tower / Feuerwachturm - Hanioti

This path takes one from Hanioti on the east coast of Kassandra up onto the long ridge, which is the backbone of the peninsula. It then follows this ridge north to the fire lookout tower, situated at one of the highest points on the ridge, before descending again to Hanioti.

The climb follows goat tracks up a minor ridge from Hanioti to reach the main ridge, which gives expansive views in all directions of the surrounding terrain. A wide forest track is followed along the middle section revealing fine views of Skioni and the western coastline and, on the descent to Hanioti, the eastern coast lies before us.

Diese Wanderung führt Sie vom Ort Hanioti an der Ostküste der Kassandra hinauf auf den langen Gebirgsrücken der Halbinsel. Dann folgt er in Richtung Norden dem Kamm zum Feurwachturm, der auf einem der höchsten Erhebungen errichtet wurde, und schließlich wieder hinunter nach Hanioti.

Der Aufstieg folgt Ziegenpfaden auf die Hügel oberhalb von Hanioti, und führt weiter auf die höchste Erhebung mit dem Wachturm. Dort können Sie den herrlichen Ausblick auf die gesamte Chalkidiki genießen. Auf der mittleren Etappe der Route wandern Sie auf einem langen Waldpfad, mit Aussicht auf Skioni und die Westseite der Küste. Beim Abstieg blicken Sie auf die Ostküste der Kassandra.

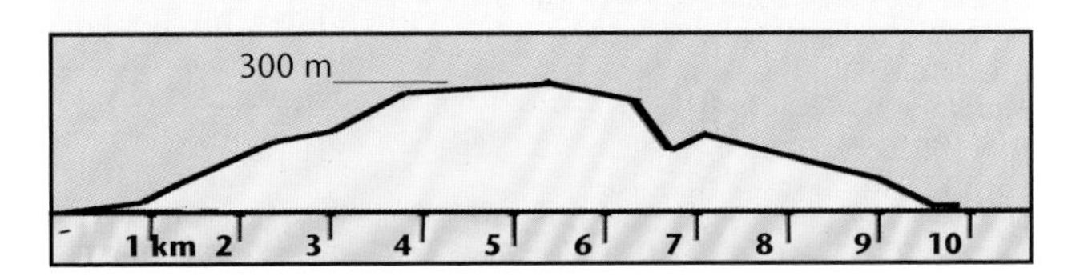

Start: From the centre of Hanioti follow the main road south for 200m and then turn right onto the road to Nea Skioni. 600m up this road, soon after passing a sign advertising the *Hotel Hilltop*, there is an open area ahead on the left, with a fountain and childrens' park. Look for steps moulded in to the side

Ausgangspunkt: Gehen Sie auf der Hauptstraße im Zentrum von Hanioti los, 200m Richtung Süden und biegen Sie dann rechts auf die Straße, die nach Nea Skioni führt. Nach 600m kommen Sie an einem Werbeplakat des *Hotel Hilltop* vorbei und kurz danach sehen Sie zu Ihrer Linken ein offenes Gelände

of the dry concrete water channel and cross to the other side. As the recreation area is reached turn left up the small track with a fenced olive grove on the left and a goat shelter on the right. At the end of the goat shelter bear right onto a sandy track which climbs up onto a minor ridge leading south. As you gain height, passing a large rock on your left, look back for a fine view of the coast Sithonia, Turtle Island and Mount Athos beyond. The route eventually becomes more wooded, as it meanders up and down along the ridge to arrive at a dirt track in a further 600m or so. Look for the continuation of the route on the opposite side of this track, about 15m to the left. The ascent continues up a dry streambed, which leads southwards and upwards, to emerge onto a broad forest road in a further 200m. Turn right onto this road and follow it for 200m. Here it is possible to leave the road and bear off to the left up a goat track. This gives a further 300m of interesting walking before it drops down once more to rejoin the forest road. Now follow this forest road for 300m, to its intersection with the main track traversing the backbone of Kassandra. Here turn right for the second leg of the journey, which leads along this broad track for 250m, at which point if crosses the road between Hanioti and Nea Skioni. The track continues in a northwesterly direction and is an ideal platform from which to view the west coast of the peninsula. The fire tower is reached after 2km of easy walking along this track. Take

mit einem Springbrunnen und einem Kinderspielplatz. Überqueren Sie auf den angelegten Stufen den trockengelegten Wasserkanal zur anderen Seite. Am Freizeitpark biegen Sie links auf einen kleinen Pfad. Zu Ihrer Linken befindet sich ein umzäunter Olivenhain und zu Ihrer Rechten ein Ziegenpferch. Am Ende des Ziegenpferches biegen Sie nach rechts auf einen Sandweg ab, der Richtung Süden in die Hügelkette hineinführt. Während Sie aufsteigen und an einem großen Felsen zu Ihrer Linken vorbeikommen, können Sie bei einem Blick rückwärts die Küste von Sithonia, die Schildkröteninsel und den Berg Athos im Hintergrund sehen.

Jetzt erreichen Sie ein Waldgebiet. Es geht auf und ab, bis Sie nach 600m auf eine ungeteerte Straße treffen. Die Route geht auf der anderen Seite der Straße, ungefähr 15m schräg nach links, weiter. Jetzt steigen Sie weiter auf einem ausgetrockneten Flußbett hinauf Richtung Süden, bis Sie nach 200m eine breite Waldstraße erreichen. Biegen Sie links auf diese Straße und folgen Sie ihr weitere 200m. Hier können Sie, wenn Sie möchten, die Straße verlassen und linkerhand auf einem Ziegenpfad aufsteigen. Das sind zusätzliche 300m Wandervergnügens!

Der Weg verbindet sich dann wieder mit der Forststraße. Gehen Sie jetzt 300m auf der Forststraße entlang, bis diese sich mit der Hauptroute kreuzt, die sich quer zum Hang bewegt, dem Rückgrat von Kassandra. Biegen Sie rechts ab. Die 2. Etappe der

the wide access track, which winds up to the tower from a point on the main track just below it.
The descent back to Hanioti passes through the field directly north of the tower to emerge into a smaller field. Follow the right hand edge of the field to arrive at another forest track. Turn right onto this track, with a wood to the left. At the end of the wood turn left down the ridge onto a track leading to a field. Continue down, past young olives to the right, along this fine grassy ridge, towards an outcrop of rock ahead. Take the path to the left of the outcrop to arrive in another large field. Follow the left-hand edge of this field first southeast and then northwest as it turns to descend into a smaller field. At the bottom of the smaller field the path continues northwest as it descends very steeply through dense brush on a goat track. The route gradually swings round to the north to arrive in a dry streambed, about 500m after leaving the ridge. A short climb up the bank on the opposite side of the streambed brings one to a

Wanderung beginnt auf dieser breiten Straße, die nach 250m die Landstraße zwischen Hanioti und Nea Skioni überquert. Der Weg führt Richtung Nordwesten weiter und bietet ideale Aussichtspunkte, um die Westküste der Halbinsel zu überblicken. Nach 2km leichter Wanderung erreichen Sie den Feuerwachturm. Nehmen Sie die Zufahrt-straße, die direkt unterhalb des Hauptpfades hinauf zum Turm führt.
Der Abstieg nach Hanioti erfolgt auf einem Pfad, der vom Turm Richtung Norden durch ein Feld auf ein anderes, kleineres Feld führt. Gehen Sie am rechten Rand des Feldes entlang, bis Sie zu einem Waldpfad kommen. Biegen Sie rechts auf den Pfad. Am Ende des Waldes, der sich zu Ihrer linken Seite befindet, biegen Sie links den Berg hinunter auf einen Weg, der in ein Weizenfeld mündet. Gehen Sie weiter abwärts, vorbei an jungen Oliven-bäumen zu Ihrer Rechten, auf dem grünen Gebirgsrücken entlang, bis zu einem Felsvorsprung. Nehmen Sie den Pfad, der links vom Felsvorsprung auf ein anderes

The fire watch tower seen from the ascent route
Feurwachturm sichtbar vom Weg

broad mountain road. Turn left onto the road and walk 100m or so up the road to a junction with a traditional brushwood goat shelter set in the 'Y' of the fork. Climb up past the right hand side of this shelter and follow the goat track up onto the next ridge. After half a kilometre of generally gentle ascent the dense brush gives way to more open country. The route now continues along the ridge in an easterly direction for a further 800m to emerge into a succession of cornfields, and the occasional olive grove, linked by a narrow track that follows the ridgeline. Follow the route markers to avoid trampling the crop when the field is sown. A further 1700m of gradual descent brings us to a large concrete water reservoir with cabin on top, complete with radio mast. From here the route descends to the village, through a grove of large pine trees, to a crossroads in the wood. Turn right here, keep left at the next junction and follow the track down to the main road in Hanioti, which is reached in a distance of 800m from the reservoir. Turn right along the road for the village centre.

Sithonia & Mt Athos
from this walk
sichtbar vom Weg

großes Feld leitet. Gehen Sie links am Rande des Feldes vorbei, zuerst in südöstliche und dann in nordwestliche Richtung, bis Sie auf einem kleineren Feld angelangen. Der Weg geht am Ende des Feldes auf einem Ziegenpfad durch die Büsche Richtung Nordwesten sehr steil hinab. Nach 500m schwenkt die Route nach Norden ab und kommt zu einem ausgetrockneten Flußbett. Steigen Sie auf der anderen Seite des Flußbettes am Ufer hoch, bis zu einer breiten Gebirgsstraße. Biegen Sie links auf diese Straße ab und gehen Sie ca. 100m bis zu einer Gabelung, wo ein ortstypischer Ziegenpferch im Unterholz steht. Steigen Sie an der rechten Seite des Pferchs vorbei auf dem Ziegenpfad zum Kamm auf. Nach einem halben Kilometer leichten Anstiegs erreichen Sie am Ende der Büsche eine flachere Kuppe. Die Route folgt jetzt ca. 800m dem Gebirgsrücken Richtung Osten, bis sie auf eine Reihe von Weizenfeldern und Olivenhainen, durch die ein enger Pfad verläuft, trifft. Folgen Sie den Wegweisern und vermeiden Sie es, wenn Saatzeit ist, auf die Saat zu treten. Nach weiteren 1,7km geradlinigem Abstiegs erreichen Sie ein großes Wasserreservoir aus Beton, mit einer Antenne auf der Betondecke. Von hier führt die Route durch einen großen Pinienwald abwärts ins Dorf. An der Kreuzung biegen Sie rechts ab, dann an der nächsten links bis Sie nach 800m auf der Hauptstraße von Hanioti ankommen. Schräg gegenüber sehen Sie die Kreuzung mit der Straße, die zur Ortsmitte führt.

Coast of Sithonia
Küste der Sithonia

The picturesque peninsula

Sithonia

Die malerische Halbinsel

Elia Beach - Ag. Pavlos Petros - Elia Beach

This high level easy route starts at the roadside just opposite the back entrance to the Athena Palace Hotel at Elia Beach. It is an easy woodland walk along forest roads and narrow tracks, which give fine views of the coastline and beyond. The walk visits the church to Paul the Apostle on the hill above Elia Beach and also Petros, the very large rock, with a trig point on its summit, which pokes up through the trees. This is the highest point on the ridge and those with a good head for heights can ascend the rock to enjoy the excellent views over the peninsula.

Ag. Paulus (The church of St Paul the Apostle) is built near an ancient spring with very pure water. You will probably observe local people here filling plastic bottles and loading them into their cars, particularly on a Sunday. The legend goes that St. Paul passed through here on his way to Rome and at this spot he was thirsty. He prayed for water and struck the ground with his staff. The spring immediately gushed forth and it has been flowing ever since.

Diese Wanderung ist eine leichte Höhenwanderung, die an der Abzweigung eines kleinen Feldwegs von der Sithonia Hauptstraße, unmittelbar hinter dem Hotel Athena Palace in Elia beginnt. Es geht auf Waldwegen und schmalen Pfaden durch das Waldgebiet. Unterwegs begleiten Sie herrliche Aussichten auf die Küste und die unberührte Landschaft. Auf dem Berg oberhalb von Elia können Sie die Kirche Apostel Paul besichtigen und ausserdem den Petros, einen großen Granit-Felsen mit hervorragender Aussicht, besteigen. Das ist der höchste Punkt auf dem Gebirgsrücken und wer trittsicher und schwindelfrei ist, kann den Felsen besteigen und die atemberaubende Sicht auf die Halbinsel genießen.

Agios Pavlos (die Kirche vom Heiligen Paul, dem Apostel) ist neben einem antiken Brunnen mit sehr klarem Wasser gebaut. Wahrscheinlich werden Sie die Einheimischen beobachten, besonders an Sonntagen, wie Sie Plastikflaschen mit Wasser füllen und in ihren Autos verstauen. Der Legende nach soll hier der Apostel Paul auf seinem Weg nach Rom vorbeigekommen sein und da er durstig war, betete er an dieser Stelle für Wasser und schlug mit seinem Stock auf den Boden. Sofort sprang eine Quelle hervor und seitdem sprudelt das Wasser.

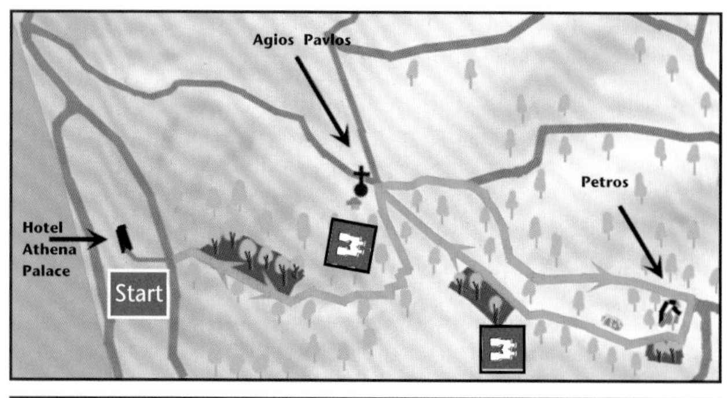

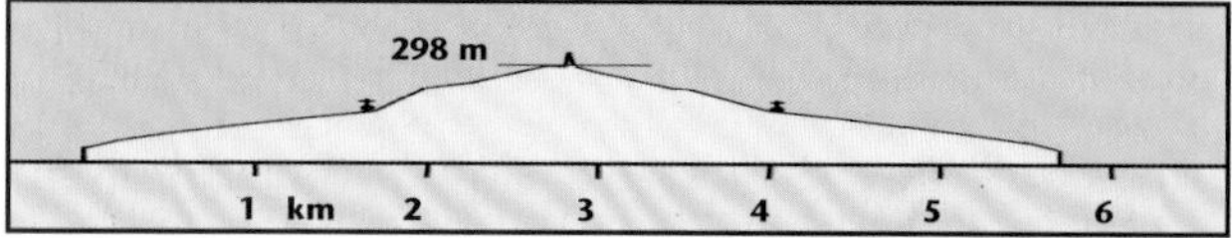

The path starts at the track, which leads into an olive grove almost directly opposite to the rear entrance of the Athena Palace Hotel. The track runs in a southeasterly direction along the edge of the olive grove for about 300m when a track junction is reached. Take the lower track, which passes an electrical sub station as it meanders along, but still continues in the same general direction. In 400m or so a shallow valley to the right gradually gets deeper and the route begins to climb more steeply through the trees in a series of short zig zags. As the broad summit of the ridge is reached, the path turns more to the north and the woodland thins, thus providing fine views over the coast. Four hundred metres of gentle ascent along this broad ridge bring the walker to Ag. Paulus, with its holy well.

The land on this plateau is like a giant rock garden as massive rocks are interspersed with pine trees, flowering shrubs, heathers, and other plants. It is beautiful at any time of the year, but even

Die Route beginnt auf dem Pfad, der in einen Olivenhain führt, direkt hinter dem Hotel Athena Palace. Der Pfad geht in südöstlicher Richtung am Rande des Olivenhains entlang und kommt nach 300m an eine Weggabelung. Gehen Sie auf dem unteren Pfad weiter, der an einer Trafo-Station vorbeiführt und in gleichbleibende Richtung schlendert. Nach 400m wird das flache Tal zu Ihrer Rechten immer tiefer und Sie beginnen zickzackförmig durch die Bäume steil aufzusteigen. Wenn Sie das oberhalb gelegene Plateau erreichen, wendet sich der Pfad nach Norden und der Wald wird lichter, so daß Sie durch die Bäume die Aussicht auf die Küste genießen können. Nach 400m leichten Anstiegs kommen Sie zur Agios Pavlos Kirche mit ihrer heiligen Quelle.

Die Landschaft auf diesem Plateau erscheint einem wie ein gigantischer Felsgarten, in dem wuchtige Felssteine mit Pinienbäumen zusammenstehen, sowie blühende Büsche, Heidekraut und

more so in the Spring. Like many other walks in the area, many of the forest tracks are lined with beehives and there is often the sweet smell of honey in the air.
To continue on to visit Petros, take the sandy track that leads almost due east from the church (Look for the way-markers). Four hundred metres along this track look out for a Poseidon waymarker on a tree to the right of the track. This marks the start of a narrow woodland path that will take us directly to Petros. The route winds through the trees and there are many tracks, due to the herds of goats that graze in these woods. To avoid getting lost, look for the Poseidon waymarkers on the trees. The track meanders on in a southeasterly direction for a distance of 300m to arrive at an open, grassy clearing in the woods surrounded by large rocks.
This is a good place to take a coffee break. The rocks in this area and the sand in the road sparkle a lot when seen in the sunshine. This is due to the presence of the mineral mica in the rocks, which is used in industry as an electrical insulator. The path now continues, through mainly open woodland, to the southeast. In 400m we emerge onto a track immediately to the north of Petros, although the rock itself is hidden amongst the trees. Follow the grassy track to the south end of the rock where there are old olive trees. Stop at the first olive tree, turn right and make for two pine trees below the southern end of the rock. The path up the rock passes between these two trees.

andere Pflanzen. Es ist zu jeder Jahreszeit wunderschön, aber natürlich besonders im Frühling. Wie auf vielen der anderen Wanderrouten, stehen Bienenstöcke in gerader Linie am Wegesrand aufgereiht und die Luft duftet nach Honig.
Um zu dem Felsen Petros zu kommen, folgen Sie dem Forstweg, der von der Kirche ostwärts führt (schauen Sie nach dem Wegweiser). Gehen Sie 400m auf diesem Weg bis zu einem Poseidon-Wegweiser, der rechts an einem Baum hängt. Hier beginnt ein schmaler Waldpfad, der Sie direkt zum Petros bringt. Die Route windet sich durch die Bäume, während viele andere Pfade zu den Weiden der Ziegenherden führen. Damit Sie sich nicht verlaufen, achten Sie immer auf die Poseidon- Wegweiser an den Bäumen. Sie wandern jetzt für etwa 300m Richtung Südosten, bis zu einer weiten, grünen Lichtung im Wald, die von Felsen umgeben ist. Hier können Sie eine Kaffeepause einlegen. Sehen Sie, wie der Sand und die Felsen bei Sonnenschein strahlen! In den Felsen befindet sich das Mineral Muskovit, das von der Industrie als Isolierstoff verwendet wird. Der Pfad führt hauptsächlich durch das Waldgebiet Richtung Südosten. Nach 400m kommen Sie auf einen Pfad, der nördlich des Felskopfs des Petros liegt, unmittelbar hinter den Bäumen. Folgen sie diesem grasbewachsenen Pfad zum südlichen Ende der Felsen, wo alte Olivenbäume stehen. Halten Sie beim ersten Olivenbaum an, biegen Sie nach rechts und gehen Sie zu den beiden Pinienbäumen am südlichen Ende der Felsen.

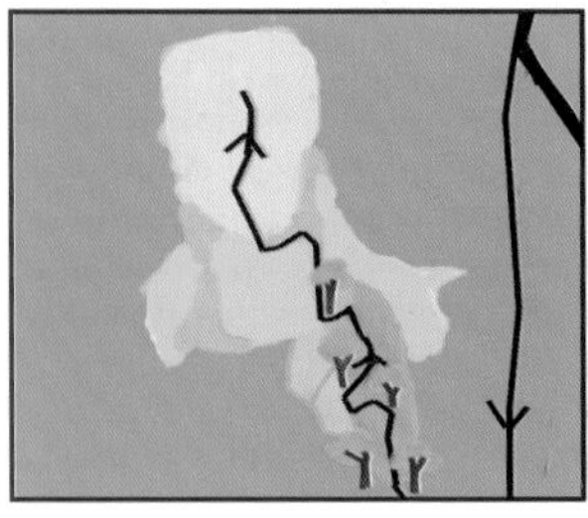

(See the inset plan of how to ascend the rock). To return to Ag. Paulus continue on through the olives (look for the waymarker) on a path leading to the northwest. On entering the wood the path soon traverses to the left, around a small hill, and a fine panoramic view is seen of the coast and Turtle Island. The route continues to descend to the northwest through the pine trees, passing a large rock face on your right. Eventually a wire fence is reached which bounds an olive grove. Continue along the fence to the join the track serving the olive grove. This track leads directly back to Ag. Paulus.
The return route from here is identical to the route of ascent.

Der Weg hinauf zum Felsen führt zwischen diesen zwei Bäumen hindurch (Details siehe Kartenausschnitt). Um zu der Ag. Pavlos Kirche zurückzukehren, gehen Sie weiter durch die Olivenbäume auf einem Pfad Richtung Nordwesten (schauen Sie nach dem Wegweiser). Sobald Sie in den Wald hineinkommen, schwenkt der Pfad nach links, um einen kleinen Hügel herum, von wo Sie schöne Aussicht auf die Küste und die Schildkröteninsel haben. Es geht weiter Richtung Nordwesten abwärts durch die Pinienbäume, vorbei an einer großen Felsnase. Schließlich erreichen Sie einen Maschendrahtzaun, der einen Olivenhain umgibt. Gehen Sie am Zaun entlang zu dem Weg, der in den Olivenhain führt. Dieser Feldweg führt direkt zu der Ag. Pavlos Kirche zurück. Der Rückweg erfolgt auf dem Ihnen bereits bekannten Weg.

Nikiti - Ag. Nikolaos - Nikiti

This walk is a circular route that uses mainly forest tracks to cross over the hill behind Nikiti to visit the small town of Ag. Nikolaus (Santa Claus). The start of the walk is beside the school in Nikiti. When coming from the north turn left at the traffic lights and find a parking place along the roadside.
The school is on the left side of this road not far from the lights

Hier handelt es sich um eine Rundwanderung, die sich hauptsächlich auf Feldwegen, durch die Hügellandschaft hinter Nikiti und um den kleinen Ort Agios Nikolaos bewegt. Ausgangspunkt ist die Schule in Nikiti. Wenn Sie aus nördlicher Richtung kommen, biegen Sie an der Ampel links ab und parken Sie Ihr Auto auf der Straße, die in das alte Dorf hineinführt.
Nicht weit von der Ampel, auf der linken Seite dieser Straße befindet sich die Schule.

Walk from here northwards up the street, past a pharmacy to crossroads. Here there is a sign to the *Old Village* pointing straight ahead. Continue on in the same direction to reach a road junction. Bear left here as the road narrows and continues to gain height, passing through the older quarter of Nikiti. Eventually the road becomes paved and quite steep as it climbs up past the fine church and the graveyard. At the crossroads beyond the church carry straight on up the hill; on the unmade road. As one climbs it is worth looking back occasionally for a view over the village. The road climbs up through trees and more open ground to reach the ridge in a further 500m or so. Turn left along the ridge track that climbs to the north,

Gehen Sie von hier nordwärts die Straße hinauf, an einer Apotheke vorbei, bis zu einer Abzweigung. Folgen Sie dem Schild mit der Aufschrift *Old Village* geradeaus, bis zu einer Kreuzung, wo Sie links abbiegen. Je höher Sie steigen, desto schmaler wird die Straße, die durch das alte Nikiti führt. Schließlich ist die Straße wieder asphaltiert und führt steil bergauf, an der Kirche vorbei, bis zu einer Gabelung mit einer unbefestigten Straße. Steigen Sie auf dieser Straße weiter auf und schauen Sie ab und zu nach hinten - die Sicht über den Ort ist sehr schön. Die Straße steigt weiter an und nach ca. 500m durch die Bäume und das offene Land erreichen Sie den Bergrücken. Biegen Sie links auf den Bergweg ab und gehen Sie nördlich auf dem Gebirgs-

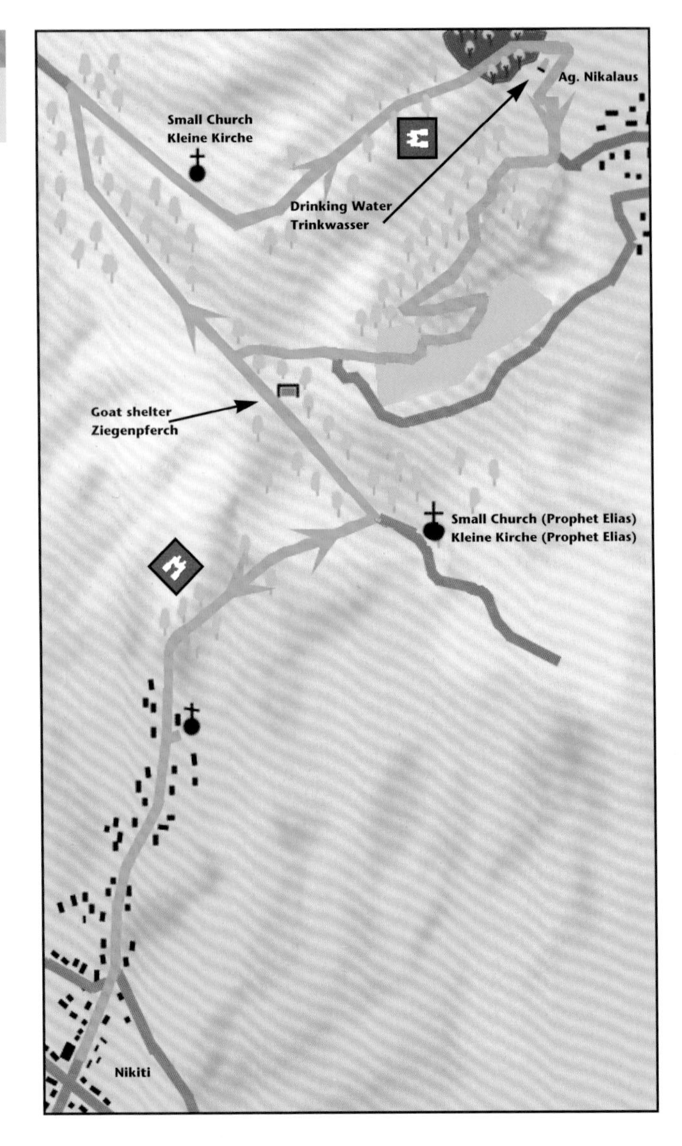
Ag. Nikalaus
Small Church
Kleine Kirche
Drinking Water
Trinkwasser
Goat shelter
Ziegenpferch
Small Church (Prophet Elias)
Kleine Kirche (Prophet Elias)
Nikiti

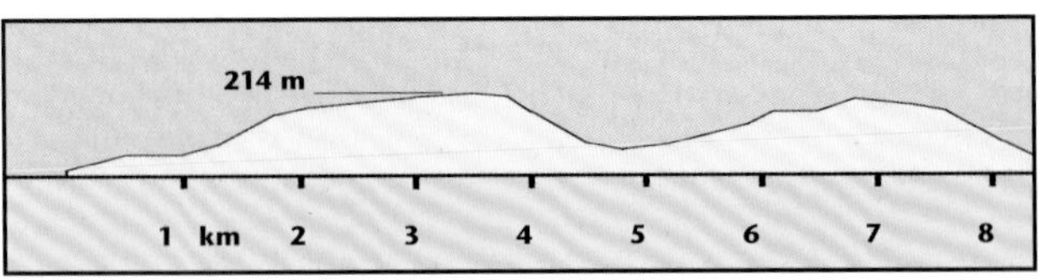
214 m
1 km 2 3 4 5 6 7 8

eventually passing a goat shelter in a field on the right. The route now enters an olive grove in much more open ground and continues to the north to arrive at a junction, with a concrete triangulation point over to the left. Keep straight on at the junction. The track continues north through open woodland and fields, with beehives lining parts of the route. After about 500m of walking a junction is reached with a road to the right, signposted *Agios Nicolaus*. Follow this track as it sweeps round to the east giving fine sea and mountain views ahead. To the right is a deep valley, which is contained by the ridge that we have walked round. Three hundred metres from the junction a small church is reached; perched on the top of the ridge with a fine view of the valley below. Here there are also picnic tables if a rest stop is in mind. Leaving the church the track crosses a small plateau and then begins to descend quite steeply towards olive groves ahead. From here our goal, the village of St. Nikolaus, can be seen over to the right, as the descent continues, on a shady woodland track, to emerge at more olive groves on both sides of the path.

Eventually the track levels out at a junction where there are beehives and a small blue Eklissaki. Turn right at the junction to arrive at a spring and water trough, fed from the hillside behind.

The track now continues in a southerly direction towards the ridge ahead, before swinging left and climbing up to the outskirts of the village, which can be seen on the left. The return route to Nikiti

rücken entlang, vorbei an einem Ziegenpferch auf dem Feld zu Ihrer Rechten. Die Route führt jetzt durch weites flaches Land zu einem Olivenhain und weiter Richtung Norden, bis zu einer Gabelung, in der links eine dreieckige Stelle aus Beton sichtbar ist. Gehen Sie geradeaus weiter, durch das Waldgebiet und die Felder, entlang an den am Wegrand aufgestellten Bienenstöcken. Nach 500m kommen Sie an eine Abzweigung, wo ein Schild mit der Aufschrift *Agios Nikolaos* in östliche Richtung weist. Im Vordergrund ist das Meer und die Berge deutlich sichtbar und zu Ihrer Rechten das tiefe Tal, das Sie gerade umgangen haben. Von der kleinen Kirche, die Sie nach 300m auf der Spitze erreichen, haben Sie einen schönen Blick auf das Tal. Hier stehen auch einige Picknicktische, für diejenigen, die eine kleine Verschnaufspause einlegen wollen. Nachdem Sie die Kirche verlassen haben, überqueren Sie ein kleines Plateau und beginnen dann einen steilen Abstieg hinunter zu den Olivenhainen. Agios Nikolaos ist schon auf der rechten Seite zu sehen. Es geht auf einem schattigen Waldweg weiter, bis auf beiden Seiten des Weges Olivenhaine erscheinen. Es wird wieder flach und Sie kommen an eine Gabelung, wo ein kleines, blaues *Eklissaki* steht. Biegen Sie rechts ab und gehen Sie bis zum Wassertrog. Der Weg führt jetzt Richtung Süden weiter auf den Berghang zu, schwenkt nach links und steigt auf zum Dorf, das auf der linken Seite zu sehen ist. Hier an der Ecke beginnt auch

starts at this corner. If you are not going into Ag. Nikolaus look for a waymarker sign to the right just on the bend of the road. This takes you into and across the mature olive grove, with a chicken hut on the left. Follow the rough chalk track past the buildings and round to the left. A narrow track now climbs up the slope to the left to meet another track. This now contours south, following the ridge above you to climb up into the wood. The reason for the lack of trees in this small valley is that it was the scene of a bad forest fire a few years ago and the vegetation has yet to fully recover. A large tortoise shell, bleached white, was lying near the track when I passed, possibly a victim of the fire.

On entering the wood and climbing to a flat grassy area the way ahead is blocked by dense vegetation. Here the path swings round through almost 180 degrees to climb out of the valley. The track climbs east for 120m or so, then swings west to climb up to ploughed fields on the plateau above. Depending on the season there may be crops in the ground, so follow the north eastern edge of the field round to meet a farm access track leading due west. In 100m this track joins another good sandy track leading south to arrive at another junction 100m on. Turn right here, following the track, to arrive back at the track junction with the concrete triangulation post nearby. From here retrace your steps to Nikiti.

der Rückweg nach Nikiti. Wenn Sie nicht nach Agios Nikolaos hinein möchten, folgen Sie dem Wegschild, das rechts am Straßenrand steht, und über einen alten Olivenhain, mit einem Hühnerstall auf der linken Seite, führt. Folgen Sie dem harten, steinigen Pfad an den Gebäuden vorbei und links herum. Auf einem schmalen Pfad steigen Sie jetzt die Bergflanke hinauf, bis zu einem anderen Pfad, der Richtung Süden auf dem Bergrücken entlang in den Wald hineinführt. Wie Sie feststellen werden, gibt es in diesem kleinen Tal kaum Bäume. Vor einigen Jahren hat ein Waldbrand hier alles zerstört und die Natur braucht einige Zeit sich erst wieder zu regenerieren. Als ich das letzte Mal auf diesem Pfad entlangging, lag ein großer, weißer Schildkrötenpanzer auf dem Weg, vermutlich ist auch die Schildkröte dem Feuer zum Opfer gefallen.

Gehen Sie durch den Wald und steigen Sie zu einer grünen Lichtung auf. Der Weg ist jetzt durch dichte Sträucher bedeckt und macht eine 180 Grad Drehung, um vom Tal hinaufzusteigen. Sie wandern 120m Richtung Osten, dann wenden Sie sich nach Westen zu den gerodeten Feldern auf der Plateauhöhe. Je nach Jahreszeit, könnte es sein, daß die Felder angesät sind, deshalb gehen Sie besser am östlichen Rand entlang, um das Feld herum, und auf einer Feldstraße Richtung Westen weiter. Nach 100m verbindet sich die Straße mit einem Feldweg, auf dem Sie Richtung Süden weitergehen und nach weiteren 100m eine

andere Gabelung sehen. Biegen Sie rechts ab. Sie kommen jetzt wieder zu der Kreuzung, wo das Betondreieck steht. Von hier geht es auf dem gleichen Weg, auf dem Sie gekommen sind, zurück nach Nikiti.

Drinking water, behind the little church to the Prophet Elias
Trinkwasser, hinter der kleinen Kirche des Propheten Elias

Neos Marmaras - Parthenonas

This long walk visits the very old village of Parthenonas and the walker is given two alternative methods of ascent and descent, depending on one's abilities. One can ascend by a beautiful, if strenuous route, which visits an old water mill and dam and then climbs straight up a ridge, through olive groves and forest, to reach high forest tracks, leading to the village. Alternatively one can ascend from the Taverna '*Drossia*' via easy forest roads. The descent can be by either of the above routes or a much shorter, steep route which follows a mountain streambed. (4 hours)

Parthenonas dates back to the days of the pirates when the inhabitants lived in the hills away from such danger. The village stands at a height of 300m and the difficulty of living there in modern times caused the whole population to abandon it in 1970, and move down en-masse into Neo Marmaras, where the living was easier. However, since then many of the houses are now being renovated, as

Bei dieser langen Wanderung besuchen Sie die alte Ansiedlung Parthenonas. Es stehen Ihnen zwei Aufstiegsvarianten zur Wahl, eine etwas steilere oder eine flachere und weniger anstrengende Route, je nach Ihrer Ausdauer.
Man kann auf einer wunderschönen, aber anstrengenden Route zu einer alten Wassermühle aufsteigen und dann weiter einem Kamm folgen, der durch Olivenhaine und Wälder auf einem alten Pfad direkt in das Dorf führt. Sie können aber auch von der Taverne Drossia auf leichten Forststraßen in das Dorf gelangen. Der Abstieg kann entweder auf einer der erstgenannten Routen erfolgen, oder auf einer kürzeren, steilen Route, die durch ein Flußtal direkt nach Neos Marmaras führt.
Dauer: 4 Stunden

Die Geschichte von Parthenonas geht zurück in die Zeit der Piraten, als die Einheimischen sich in den Bergen vor ihnen versteckten. Das Leben in dem Dorf, das sich in 300m Höhe befindet, war nicht leicht. Deshalb verließ die ganze Bevölkerung bis 1970 das Dorf und zog nach Neos Marmaras.
Wie dem auch sei, in den letzten Jahren wurden in Parthenonas ein kleines Hotel

wealthier people move back for the fine views, peace and solitude.

und zwei Tavernen eröffnet und viele Häuser werden von den wohlhabenden Besitzern, die hier die herrliche Aussicht, Ruhe und Einsamkeit suchen, renoviert.

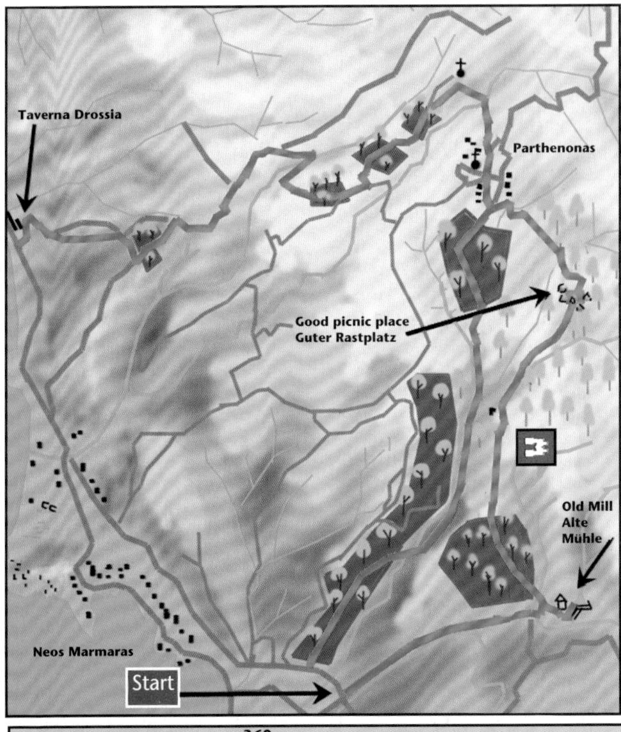

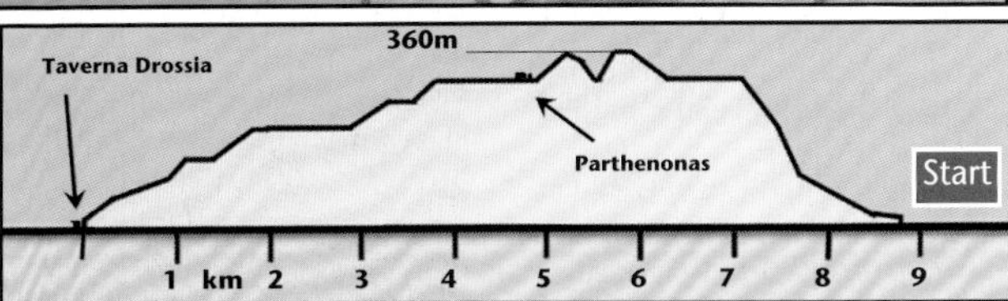

Option A : Strenuous
Direct ascent, including the visit to an old watermill. The walk starts on the Neos Marmaras bypass directly opposite the southern access road into the village, the

Vorschlag A: anstrengende Wanderung. Direkter Aufstieg, mit Besichtigung der alten Wassermühle. Die Wanderung beginnt bei der Umgehungsstraße von Neos Marmaras, direkt gegenüber der südlichen

Porto Carras end.
At the start, look for the waymarker marking a farm access track directly opposite the southern access to Neos Marmaras. This track descends from the road and continues in a northeasterly direction, for 600m or so, to arrive at a farm, with cattle and pigs. Further on beehives are passed. About here we leave the farm track, joining a smaller path to the right, which continues, towards the head of the valley. Soon a streambed is crossed, and then crossed again, as the route bears round towards the south. The path now follows the left bank of the stream for 200m, to arrive at an abandoned mill. Although it only dates back to the 1920's this building is worth investigating. A path to the left of the building leads up and behind it to a large water storage tank. A 160m long stone aqueduct, which can be followed up the valley to the dam and reservoir, feeds this tank. To continue to Parthenonas we retrace our steps from the mill for 60m. Here turn right, at a large olive tree, onto a path which climbs the ridge on which the olive grove stands. The route continues upwards for more than a kilometre, negotiating the stepped levels of the olive grove.
As you climb take time to enjoy the view of Turtle Island to the rear, the fine olive groves to the left and the deep gorge that drops away to your right. Eventually the olive grove is left behind and the path passes through shrubland and. forest, meandering somewhat, but maintaining its line up the

Einfahrtsstraße zum Ort.
Suchen Sie nach der Wegmarkierung am Zufahrtsweg zu einem Bauernhof, gegenüber der Südeinfahrt von Neos Marmaras. Dieser Weg führt nach Nordosten. Nach ca. 600m kommen Sie zu einem Bauernhof mit Rindern und Schweinen. Nachdem Sie an Bienenstöcken vorbeigegangen sind, biegen Sie rechts auf einen kleineren Weg ab, der auf den Talschluß zuführt. Nach einer Weile überqueren Sie zweimal das Flußbett und folgen der Route Richtung Süden. Der Weg führt jetzt am linken Flußufer entlang und kommt nach etwa 200m an die verlassene Mühle. Obwohl sie nur auf 1920 zurückdatiert wird, lohnt es sich, die Mühle näher zu besichtigen. Der linke Pfad führt hinter das Gebäude, zu einem großen Wasserspeicher. Das Wasser wird durch eine 160m lange,

The old mill
Die alte Mühle

The Water leat
Die Wasserleitung

ridge. At the top of a rise, a farm is seen ahead. The path now swings due north to avoid the farm, and turns on to a farm track. This track travels northeast through open woodland and across a narrow ridge, with a gorge on both sides. As you cross the ridge look for two large stones at the left of the track. The path leaves the farm road here to continue its journey to the head of the valley. The way now passes through a small canyon, beyond which is a flat piece of ground surrounded by large rocks; a fine place for a coffee break.
The next part of the route exits at the north end of the clearing, descending to the northeast, where a flat bed of rock marks the head of the valley. The track now climbs

steinerne Wasserleitung, die durch das Tal zum Damm und zum Wasserreservoir führt, geleitet. Gehen Sie jetzt wieder ungefähr 60m zurück, damit Sie sich wieder auf den Weg ins Dorf machen. Biegen Sie an einem großen Olivenbaum rechts ab und steigen Sie auf einem Pfad den Berg hoch, wo sich ein Olivenhain befindet. Die Route geht mehr als einen Kilometer aufwärts, von Baumreihe zu Baumreihe.
Nehmen Sie sich beim Aufstieg Zeit und genießen Sie die Aussicht auf die Schildkröteninsel im Hintergrund, die schönen Olivenhaine zu Ihrer linken und die tiefe Schlucht zu Ihrer rechten Seite. Jetzt haben Sie den Olivenhain hinter sich gelassen und wandern durch Büsche und Bäume geradlinig auf die höchste Erhebung zu. Auf dem Kamm angekommen sehen Sie vor sich einen Ziegenstall. Der Weg führt jetzt Richtung Norden, um den Ziegenstall zu umgehen und kommt auf einen Feldweg. Dieser Feldweg führt nordostwärts durch das offene Waldgebiet und auf einem schmalen Gebirgsrücken zwischen zwei Schluchten hindurch. Achten Sie auf zwei große Steine zu Ihrer linken Seite. Hier verlassen Sie den Feldweg und begeben sich weiter auf einen Weg zum Talschluß. Der Weg führt jetzt durch einen kleines Tal hindurch. Dahinter befindet sich umringt von Steinen eine kleine Lichtung. Eine gute Gelegenheit für eine Kaffeepause!
Am nördlichen Ende der Lichtung geht der Weg weiter Richtung Nordosten, wo ein flacher Steinboden das Tal kennzeichnet. Es geht wieder leicht bergauf, unter einem

slightly, passing under a large tree and round a large rock. Below and to the left look for a grassy forest track. Drop down onto this track, which follows the hillside round towards the northwest for a kilometre or so, to arrive at an isolated house with beehives. Soon Parthenonas can be seen ahead as the last 600m of path leads us first down and then up to the plateau on which the village stands.

Option B: Easy

The start for this walk is the Taverna Drossia, which is on the left as you approach Neos Marmaras from the north, about 1.5km from the village. Walk up behind the taverna onto a track which rises to the left, through a small grove of olives, to meet another track. Join this track which climbs up, behind the houses and passes some beehives. Keep left at the junction as the track ascends. Continue on the main track, which meanders up in a northeasterly direction; keeping to the left at the next two intersections. The terrain alternates between olive groves and mixed woodlands and is particularly beautiful in Autumn. At the next junction keep left through the olive grove and continue, contouring round the side of a deep valley on the right, to arrive at the next fork. Here take the smaller track to the left and continue on through an olive grove on a broad, flat plateau of land for 200m or so, when the path begins to climb again. At the next junction follow the lower road to the right as the road to the left is just an access road for a small church on the hillside above. From here one gets a

großen Baum weiter und um einen großen Felsen herum. Sie sehen links unten eine grasbewachsene Forststraße. Gehen Sie auf ihm ungefähr einen Kilometer um den Berg herum bis zu einem alleinstehenden Haus mit Bienenstöcken. Nach 600m ist das Plateau, auf dem sich der Ort Parthenonas befindet, zu erkennen.

Vorschlag B: leichte Wanderung. Ausgangspunkt für diese Wanderung ist die Taverne Drossia, die sich 1,5km nördlich vor Neos Marmaras auf der linken Straßenseite befindet. Gehen Sie hinter der Taverne den Pfad entlang, der links abzweigt und nach dem kleinen Olivenhain auf einen anderen Pfad trifft. Auf diesem Weg gehen Sie bergauf an den Häusern vorbei, biegen Sie nach links und steigen sie weiter auf dem Hauptweg auf, der Richtung Nordosten führt. An den zwei Kreuzungen halten Sie sich immer links. Das Landschaftsbild wechselt von Olivenhainen in Wald über und ist im Herbst besonders schön. Auch an der nächsten Kreuzung halten Sie sich links und gehen durch ein Olivenhain und um ein tiefes Tal auf der rechten Seite herum, bis Sie an die nächste Gabelung kommen. Folgen Sie dem kleineren Pfad zu Ihrer rechten und wandern Sie durch einen Olivenhain auf einem breiten, flachen Plateau etwa 200m, bis es wieder aufwärts geht. An der nächsten Kreuzung führt ein Weg hinauf zu einer kleinen Kirche. Sie nehmen aber den rechten Weg Richtung Nordosten. Von hier oben haben Sie eine herrliche Aussicht über das Tal von Parthenonas. Kein Wunder, daß

good view across the valley to Parthenonas and one can see how its position, high in the hills, would dissuade pirates and other marauders from venturing up there. The track continues to ascend to the northeast, then turns right at the head of the valley to ford a stream and travel southeast into Parthenonas, past a row of houses. There are two tavernas in Parthenonas, one at each end of the village. Just over the road from the Village Hall, near a large tree, is a small distillery that makes Tsipouro the local Greek firewater.

Direct Descent : This steep but safe descent brings one out on the Neos Marmaras road near the start of the strenuous route, described earlier.

From the southern end of Parthenonas, follow the Poseidon signs south, directly down through the olive groves to the stream bed. Here a goat track is followed parallel to the streambed for about 1 km, at which point the path crosses the stream into the olive grove on the other side. The route now descends through the olive grove to arrive at the main road only 300m north of the start point.

sich die Piraten und anderen Plünderer nicht wagten, das Dorf hier oben zu überfallen! Am Talschluß biegen Sie rechts ab, watten durch einen Bach und gehen geradewegs an einer Reihe von Häusern vorbei in das Dorf hinein. Es gibt zwei Tavernen in Parthenonas, jeweils am Rande des Dorfes. Gegenüber dem Rathaus, neben der großen Platane ist eine Schnapsbrennerei. Hier wird Tsipouro, ein für die Region typischer Tresterbrand, hergestellt.

Direkter Abstieg: Dieser etwas steilere, aber sichere Abstieg führt südlich des Zentrums von Neos Marmaras auf die Landstraße zurück, in der Nähe des Ausgangspunktes der anderen Route.

Am südlichen Rand des Dorfes geht ein Weg direkt hinunter zu den Olivenhainen und dem Flußbett. Folgen Sie den Poseidon Zeichen. Etwa 1km lang verläuft parallel zum Flußbett ein Ziegenpfad durch die Waldschlucht. Am Ende der Schlucht überqueren Sie das Flußbett auf die andere Seite und kommen durch einen Olivenhain zurück zur Hauptstraße, 300m nördlich des Ausgangspunktes der ersten Route.

Left: The village of Parthenonas

Links: Das Dorf Parthenonas

Porto Carras - Vineyards / Weinberge - Porto Carras

This walk from Porto Carras takes us up into the vineyards high above the Neos Marmaras, giving fine views over the sea. The return path drops to the coast, and meanders through open forest passing several beautiful sandy coves, with fine beaches, along the way.

D i e s e Wanderung führt Sie von Porto Carras hinauf zu den Weinbergen über dem Ort. Von dort oben haben Sie eine herrliche Aussicht auf das Meer. Auf dem Rückweg steigen Sie zum Meer ab, wandern durch schönen Wald und kommen unterwegs an einigen, der schönsten Buchten und Strände der Sithonia vorbei.

This walk visits the vineyards of Porto Carras below, the large house high on the hill, which looks out over the bay. It was built by the late Jannis Carras, who had a dream to bring tourism to Halkidiki. Jannis, who was educated in America, the holiday resort of Porto Carras, the first such venture in Halkidiki. This development was very important as it brought large scale tourism to Halkidiki for the first time.

Diese Wanderung führt durch die Weinberge von Porto Carras, die sich unterhalb des schloßähnlichen Ansitzes von Jannis Carras, über die Hänge bis zum Meer ziehen. Dieses aussergewöhnliche Haus war einst Wohnsitz von Jannis Carras, einem der Pioniere des Tourimus auf Chalkidiki. Nachdem er in Amerika studiert hatte, baute er die Hotelanlage von Porto Carras, das erste Unternehmen dieser Art in Chalkidiki. Es war ein großer Erfolg und zum ersten Mal kamen Touristen aus aller Welt in diese Region.

The vegetation along the tracks on this walk is particularly varied. Many wild flowering and fruiting bushes are to be found, considerably adding to the interest of the route.

Die Vegetation auf den Wanderpfaden ist äußerst vielseitig. Sie werden viele, wilde Blumen und früchtetragende Pflanzen finden, dies macht diese Wanderung noch zusätzlich interessant.

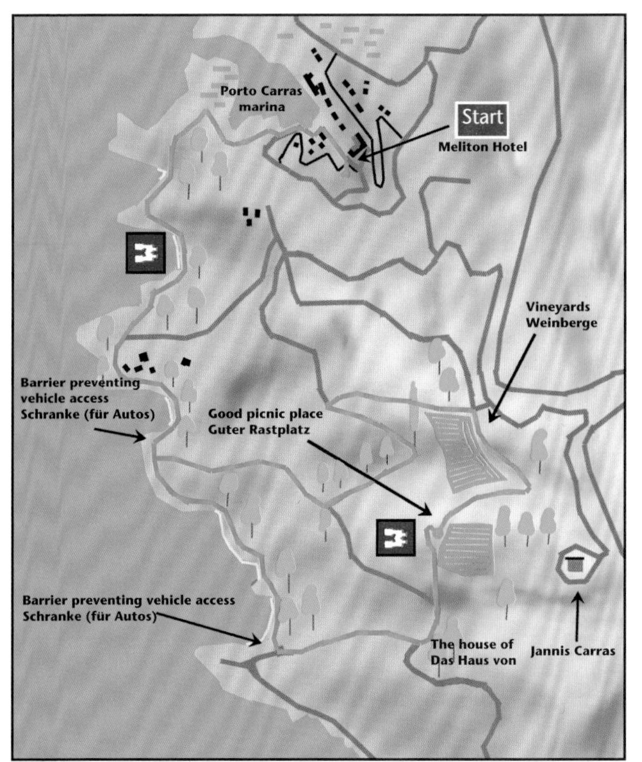

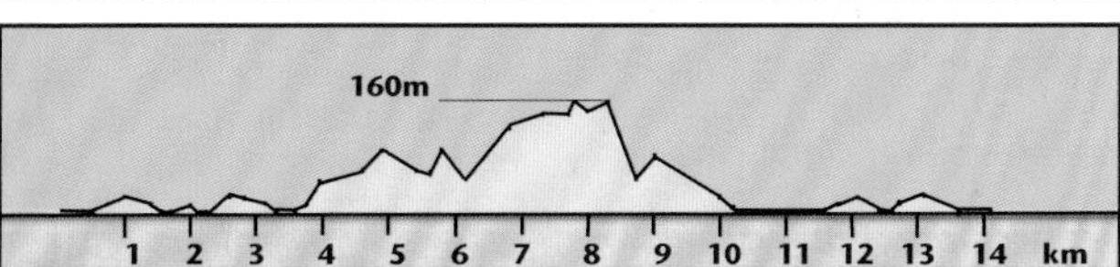

The start is reached by taking the road that bears round to the left of the Marina. Look for the sign *Marina Village Inn*. The Meliton Hotel can be seen over to the right. The road ends with a roundabout in an open area with parking space.

From the car park walk eastwards between buildings towards the Marina, In about 300m you will pass the *Gina Bachauer Hause* on your right. The path skirts round to the left of the Marina, passing

Vom Parkplatz aus gehen Sie ostwärts zwischen den Gebäuden in Richtung Marina. Nach 300m sehen Sie das *Gina Bachauer Haus* zu Ihrer rechten. Der Weg führt entlang der Marina, durch ein Wäldchen hindurch und vorbei am *Oasis Cafe*. Jetzt steigt er an und biegt auf dem ersten Hügel nach Westen. Dann fällt er wieder und führt entlang einer kleinen Bucht mit Sandstrand. Weitere kleine Sandbuchten folgen in Richtung Süden, bis

Porto Carras Marina

through a grove of trees, and going past the Oasis café. The track now climbs and turns to the left at its highest point to descend and curve round a small cove with a sandy beach. This meandering progress continues in a southerly direction round several more fine coves until at the brow of a small hill, a Porto Carras fire warning notice here marks the forest track, which leads off to the right of another track. The route now descends the hill with fine sea views to the right. In 200m a sharp turn left reveals another fine cove below and to the right. Pass by a metal barrier across the road here and continue along the route for 100m as it climbs and curves round to the left. Look for the waymarker on the left side of the road which marks the small track leading up the slope in a southwesterly direction. In 100m the track turns left into a field. Turn right and continue upwards across the field in an easterly direction to meet a track again, which leads northeast. The large house can be seen directly ahead, perched on its ledge, high above the trees. The path carries on for another 300m in the same direction to arrive at its

Sie auf einer kleinen Bergkuppe ein Schild, das vor Waldbränden warnt, sehen. Dieser Weg führt den Hügel hinunter und bietet schöne Aussicht auf das glasklare Meer. Nach 200m sehen Sie nach einer scharfen Linkskurve eine weitere Bucht. Gehen Sie an einer Metallschranke vorbei und wandern Sie weitere 100m bergauf und nach links. Schauen Sie nach den Wegweisern auf der linken Seite der Straße, die auf den kleinen Pfad Richtung Südwesten hinweisen. Sie gehen einen Hang hinauf und nach 100m biegt der Pfad nach links auf ein Feld. Gehen Sie rechts über das Feld in östliche Richtung und folgen Sie einem weiteren Weg Richtung Norden. Das große Haus ist direkt oberhalb zu sehen. Es steht auf dem Felsvorsprung hoch über den Bäumen. Der Pfad geht noch weitere 300m in die gleiche Richtung, bis er seinen höchsten Punkt erreicht hat und parallel zu einer Asphaltstraße verläuft.

Hier müssen Sie auf der Asphaltstraße (es gibt keinen anderen Weg) eine tiefe Schlucht zu Ihrer linken Seite umgehen, bis Sie den Gegenhang auf der anderen Seite erreichen. Die Route geht wieder bergab Richtung Nordosten. Auf der rechten Seite sehen Sie seltene Pflanzen, auf der linken Seite eine beeindruckende Schlucht. Nach 400m erreichen Sie eine scharfe Linkskurve mit einem Zypressenbaum, der in der zweiten Kurve der Biegung Wache steht. Die Straße steigt leicht nach Osten an und nach 250m zeigt ein Wegschild auf der rechten

highest point, adjacent to a tarmac road on the left. Here we must cross onto the road (there is no other way), in order to go round the deep gorge to the left and reach the slopes on the far side. The road descends, to the north east with fine vegetation on the right and an impressive gorge to the left. In 400m, it swings sharp left around the neck of the gorge, passing a single Saeulan Cupressus, standing sentinel at the second corner of the bend. The road climbs gently east and in about 250m look for the waymarker sign on the right. This marks the continuation of the path which climbs the hillside, in an easterly direction; an about turn of nearly 180 degrees. A steep climb of 200m, with vines on the slope to our right, brings us to crossroads. Turn right here and cross above the vineyard to the other side of the valley. The track first descends, then rises to a viewpoint, then descends again, before rising again to another viewpoint, directly below the house on the hill above. There are vineyards to the left and in front of us here, with expansive views in all directions. To descend

Seite den Pfad, der ostwärts den Berg hinaufführt. So macht der Weg ein Kurve von fast 180 Grad. Dann steigen Sie 200m auf, während Sie zu Ihrer rechten die Weinreben sehen, bis Sie zu einer Kreuzung kommen. Biegen Sie rechts ab und überqueren Sie den Weinberg bis zur anderen Seite des Tals. Der Pfad fällt zuerst leicht und dann steigt er wieder auf zu einem Aussichtspunkt. Nach einem weiteren Auf und Ab erreichen Sie einen zweiten Aussichtspunkt direkt unter dem Haus auf dem Berg. Sie stehen mitten in den Weinbergen und haben einen Ausblick in alle Richtungen. Wandern Sie ein paar Meter auf dem gleichen Weg abwärts und nehmen Sie dann den Pfad, der nach links biegt und durch den Weinberg führt. Gehen Sie an der rechten Seite der Weinreben entlang bis zu einer Straße, 250m weiter unten. Folgen Sie dieser Straße, die zuerst Richtung Südosten und dann nach Westen führt. Auf diesem Abstieg gibt es herrliche Ausblicke und viel Interessantes aus der lokalen Pflanzen- und Tierwelt zu entdecken. Nach 750m

Turtle Island from the Porto Carras walk
Die Schildkröteninsel von der Porto Carras Wanderung

retrace your steps for a few metres and take the track which curves to the left and drops down through the vineyard. Walk down the right hand side of the plantation to reach the road about 250m below. Join this road, which leads south east initially but eventually curves round to the west. There are fine views and varied plant and animal life all along this descent, which joins a tarmac road after 750m or so. Bear left onto the road and follow it down for 300m, until it bends sharply to the left as it reaches the coast. Look for the waymarker which indicates the path to the right; through the trees onto a gated forest road. The path now follows this road as it meanders through the forest, always staying near to the coast and passing several small coves with fine beaches along the way. After 500m or so look for the grove of mandarin orange trees on your right. Further on, to the right, there are olive groves and a fire watch tower. There is also a lovely tree shaded beach, signed: *For the residents of Porto Carras only.* The concrete wharf across the small bay here is actually a helicopter landing pad. The track eventually arrives back at the blue fire warning notice. From here we must retrace our steps the final two kilometres back to Porto Carras.

biegen Sie nach links auf eine Asphaltstraße, die nach 300m links den Strand erreicht. Schauen Sie nach dem Wegschild, das auf den Weg nach rechts hinweist. Gehen Sie auf ihm durch den lichten Wald bis zu einer Schranke vor einer Forststraße. Folgen Sie der Forststraße durch den Wald. Bleiben Sie immer in der Nähe des Strandes. Unterwegs treffen Sie auf viele, kleine Sandbuchten mit schönen Stränden. Nach 500m sehen Sie einen Zitrusbaumhain auf der rechten Seite und etwas weiter einen Feuerwachturm. Dort gibt es auch einen sehr schönen, schattigen Strand mit dem Hinweis: *Nur für Gäste von Porto Carras.* Die Betonplatform am Ende der kleinen Bucht ist eigentlich ein Landeplatz für Hubschrauber. Die Forststraße kommt schließlich zum Waldbrand-Schild zurück. Von hier gehen Sie die letzten 2km auf dem gleichen Weg, auf dem Sie gekommen sind, wieder zurück nach Porto Carras.

Porto Carras Vineyards
Weinberge bei Porto Carras

A beach on the Porto Carras walk
Ein Strand auf der Porto Carras Wanderung

Porto Koufo - Kapros - Porto Koufo

This easy walk starts at the beautiful natural harbour of Porto Koufo on the west coast of Sithonia. The route uses farm and goat tracks to reach Kapros the remote southern peak of the peninsula.

The path passes through an area rich in flora and fauna and fine views can be obtained from Kapros of the precipitious cliffs along the coast. On a fine day the Sporades Islands can be seen to the southwest.

Porto Koufo featured in recent history. The fine natural harbour with its very deep waters made it an excellent base for the German U-boats based in the Eastern Mediterranean. Remains of a concrete water reservoir and anti-aircraft gun platforms can still be seen on the summit of Kapros.

Diese leichte Wanderung beginnt am natürlichen Hafen von Porto Koufo, an der Westküste der Sithonia. Es geht auf Feldwegen und Ziegenpfaden zum Berg Kapros, an der abgelegenen Südspitze der Halbinsel.

Der Pfad führt durch ein Gebiet, das reich an Flora und Fauna ist, und bietet herrliche Aussicht vom Kapros aus auf die steilen Klippen entlang der Küste. Bei klarem Wetter kann man die Inselgrupe der Sporaden im Südwesten sehen.

Porto Koufo wird in der Neugeschichte erwähnt. Der schöne, natürliche Hafen mit seiner großen Tiefe, war ein ausgezeichneter Stützpunkt für die deutschen U-Boote, die im Osten des Mittelmeeres stationiert waren. Die Reste eines Wasserreservoirs aus Beton und die Platform der Flugabwehrkanonen sind noch auf dem Gipfel von Kapros zu sehen.

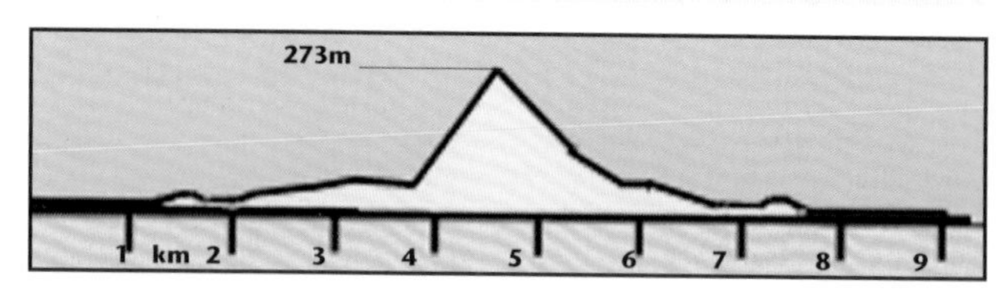

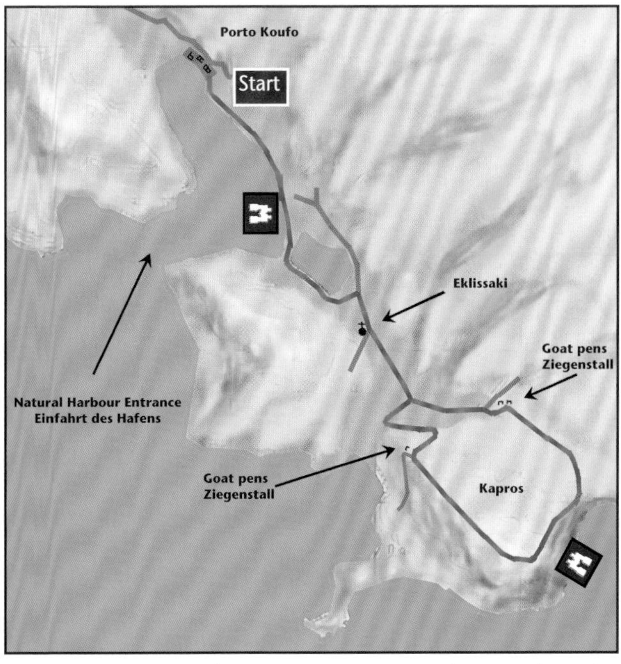

From the minor road giving access to the harbour, walk in an easterly direction along the harbour road, past the pleasure craft at their moorings. At the end of the stone jetty continue along the road until it veers away from the shoreline. To the right can be seen the wide entrance to this harbour, bounded by high rocky cliffs. Now follow the shoreline, which turns towards the south until, after walking a total distance of about 1500m from the start, the southern limit of the harbour is reached and the path climbs gently eastwards, round the lower slopes of the hill in front. Another sheet of water appears on the left as the path meanders along through thorny scrub, gradually turning east to pass between the water and an olive grove. About 350m after

Gehen Sie auf der Nebenstraße, die zum Hafen führt, Richtung Osten zu der Hafenstraße, die an der Anlegestelle für die Jachten entlangführt. Am Ende des Betonstegs folgen Sie weiter der Straße, bis Sie vom Ufer wegführt. Auf der rechten Seite sehen Sie den breiten Eingang zum Hafen, umgeben von hohen Fels-klippen. Jetzt gehen Sie am Ufer entlang, 1500m Richtung Süden, bis Sie am Südende des Hafens ankommen und der Pfad Sie langsam Richtung Osten hinaufführt, um die kleinen, vorausliegenden Hänge herum. Während Sie sich durch das dornige Gebüsch schlengeln, erscheint zu Ihrer linken eine andere Wasserfläche. Der Weg dreht nach Osten und führt zwischen dem Wasser und

leaving the harbour a dirt road is reached. The walk follows this track as it rises to the southeast through scrub, woodland and the occasional olive grove. In 200m the track rises to a minor summit, marked by a substantial white stone *Eklissaki* (little church). Looking back to Porto Koufo a fine view of the village and harbour can be seen. The track now descends, winding gradually down the hillside and turning to the east, with olives to the left and cows grazing the scrubland to the right. After 400m of gradual descent it rises again to reach old farm buildings with goat pens behind. Our route continues to follow this dirt road, which gradually turns to the south as it rises up the hillside that bounds the right side of the valley. It then turns to the east to reach, about 100m after leaving the farm buildings, a point overlooking the sea below, on a cliff 65m high. This, however, is not the final destination. The path now bears off to the right, climbing up the cliff side to reach a summit and viewpoint in another 500m or

The high cliffs of Kapros
Die hohen Klippen bei Kapros

einem Olivenhain hindurch. 350m vom Hafen entfernt kommen Sie auf eine ungeteerte Straße, die ostwärts durch das Gebüsch, den Wald und ab und zu durch einen Olivenhain führt. Nach 200m kommen Sie auf einem kleinen Hügel an, wo ein weissgetünchtes *Eklissaki* (kleine Kapelle) steht. Wenn Sie zurückblicken, haben Sie einen prächtigen Ausblick auf Porto Koufo und seinen Hafen. Der Pfad führt jetzt geradeaus die Böschung hinunter und dreht nach Osten, vorbei an Olivenbäumen zu Ihrer Linken und Gebüsch zu Ihrer Rechten. Nach 400m steigt der Pfad wieder etwas an und erreicht einen Punkt mit alten Bauernhäusern, hinter denen Ziegenställe stehen. Folgen Sie nun der Straße, die nach Süden biegt und den Hang, der das Tal auf der rechten Seite abgrenzt, hinaufführt. 100m von den Bauernhöfen entfernt, biegen Sie nach Osten und kommen auf eine 100m hohe Klippe, von der Sie auf das Meer hinunterblicken können. Sie sind aber noch nicht am Ende der Wanderung angekommen. Der Weg steigt weiter zu Ihrer Rechten, den felsigen Hang hinauf und kommt nach ca. 500m auf dem Gipfel an. Hier können Sie rasten und die wundervolle Aussicht auf das 200m unterhalb liegende Meer genießen.
Zurück geht es Richtung Norden. Sie kommen an eine Weggabelung, wo sich Ziegenpferche befinden. Nehmen Sie den Weg, der nach rechts den Hang hinunterführt und wieder auf die Aufstiegsroute leitet. Von hier geht es auf dem gleichen Weg, wie Sie gekommen

so. This is a fine place to rest and enjoy the magnificent views and the dramatic vertical drops to the sea 200m below.
To return continue on to the north to arrive at a path junction, with goat shelters just beyond. Take the path to the right which curves down the ridge to join the outward route. From here we must just retrace our steps back to Porto Koufo. There is no viable alternative route.

sind, wieder zurück nach Porto Koufo.

A group of walkers on the Porto Koufo route
Eine Wandergruppe auf der Porto Koufo Route

Sikia - Circular walk Rundwanderung - Sikia

This walk takes one on a circular trip around the ridge directly above the town to the north, giving fine views over the town and the surrounding countryside.
The route makes use of old charcoal burners paths, goat tracks and unsurfaced farm access roads.
Parts of the circuit involve rather steep, but safe, rocky ascents and descents.
Time required:- 4 hours

The Sikians have a long standing tradition of independence and an unwillingness to be subdued.

Bei dieser Route handelt es sich um eine Rundwanderung über die Berge, die nördlich den Ort umgeben. Es bieten sich herrliche Ausblicke auf den Ort und die Umgebung.
Die Route führt über alte Köhlerwege, Ziegenpfade und Feldwege.
Teilweise werden Sie auf dieser Rundwanderung über steile, aber ungefährliche Felsen auf- und absteigen.
Dauer: 4 Stunden

Die Bewohner von Sikia wahrten seit eh und je ihre Unabhängigkeit, indem sie gegen jegliche Unterdrücker Widerstand leisteten.

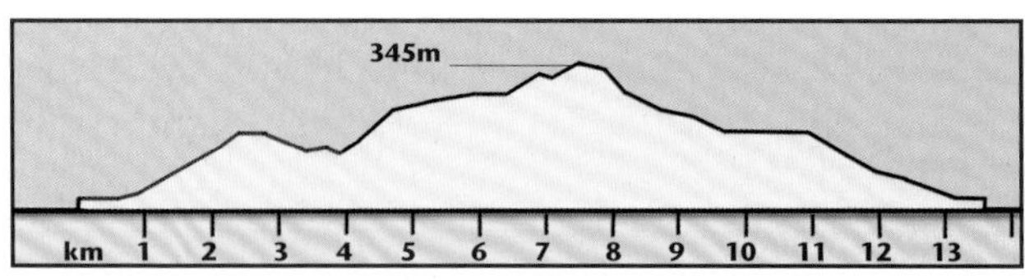

Park on the outskirts of the village, just before the one way street leading to the centre. A taverna straddles the space between the access and exit roads from the village centre. From here walk along the one way street towards the centre, with a streambed to the right.
From the Plaza look for the Poseidion waymarker signs

Parken Sie am Rande des Dorfes, kurz vor der Einfahrtstraße, die in das Dorf hineinführt. Eine Taverne steht genau zwischen der Ein- und Ausfahrtstraße des Dorfes. Gehen Sie von hier aus auf der Einfahrtstraße an einem Flußbett entlang in die Dorfmitte. Auf dem Dorfplatz steht ein Poseidon-Wegweiser, der in nördliche Richtung

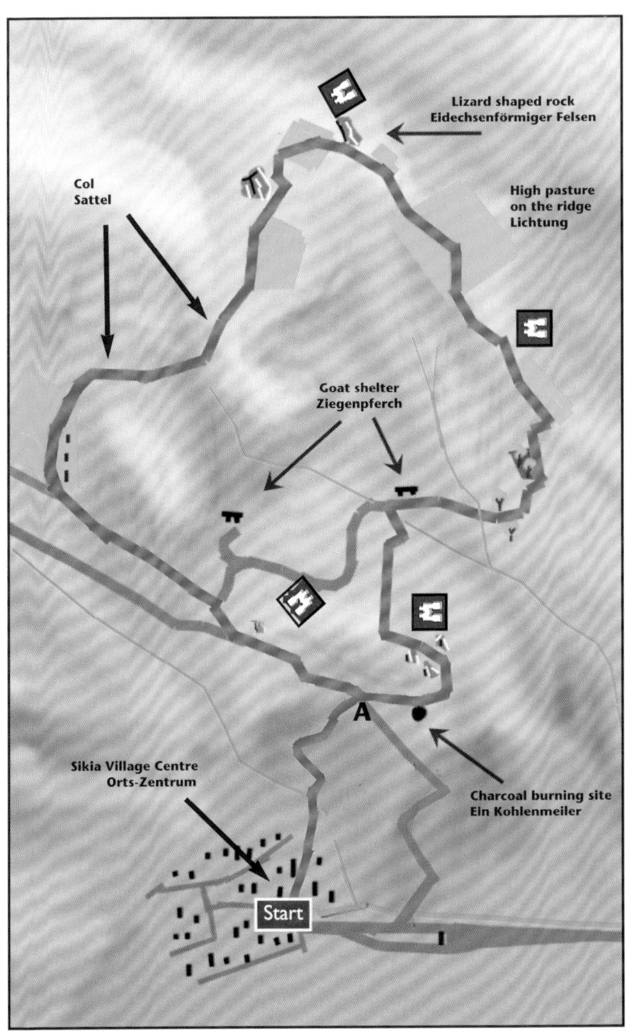

which follow the street to the northeast. At the end of the street a track continues up the hillside in a northeasterly direction, to emerge on a broad dirt road in a distance of 1 km (point **A** on the map). Cross over the road and look here for a red Poseidon sign, in spray paint, on the rock face. This marks the start of a small rocky

weist. Am Ende der Straße geht ein Pfad weiter hinauf, auf den Berghang Richtung Nordosten, bis Sie nach 1km auf eine breite, ungeteerte Straße kommen (Punkt **A** auf der Landkarte). Überqueren Sie die Straße und schauen Sie nach einem roten Poseidon-zeichen, mit Farbe auf einen Stein gesprüht. Hier beginnt ein kleiner, steiler Hang hinauf

track, that rises up the cliff face to eventually reach the summit above us.
Follow this track, which leads up to a circular grassy area in 120m or so. This is an old charcoal burner's workplace*. In former times this hill would be covered by woodland, which was felled to produce charcoal, leaving the scrubland which we see today. The path leads on, climbing up and round the end of a large rocky outcrop. It then turns northwest, leading straight up the slope, as it winds its way between, and sometimes up and over, magnificent, smooth, rounded rocks. It then turns north through a narrow col to arrive at the first summit. From here there are excellent views towards the coast and of the town and countryside below.
From the top of the hill, goat pens can be seen to the north in the valley below. Beyond is an encircling ridge, which is our next goal. Follow the goat tracks down the minor ridge which leads towards the pens (the best route should be marked with red and white tape on the bushes or red paint on the rocks).
In 500m a stream bed is crossed and the path rises to the goat pens. Walk along the farm track, which leads due east through the pens, to reach a small promontory; looking down onto a stream below.
Ahead, across the stream, are two olive trees that mark the path up the hill. Cross the stream and join the path, which climbs steeply to the east, then swings to the west, gaining 50m or so in height, to arrive at an old olive grove. The route passes through the

auf den Berggipfel.
Folgen Sie diesem Weg bis Sie nach 120m zu einer umzäunten Grünfläche kommen. Hier haben die Köhler gearbeitet. Wo jetzt nur Gebüsch zu sehen ist, war früher ein dichtes Waldgebiet, das aber von den Köhlern zwecks Holzkohlengewinnung gefällt wurde.
Dann wandern Sie nach Nordwesten, immer geradeaus und zwischen prachtvollen, glattgerundeten Felsen hindurch. Der Weg führt jetzt nordwärts, durch einen engen Pass hindurch, auf den ersten Berggipfel. Von hieraus haben Sie eine herrliche Aussicht auf die Küste der Sithonia und den Ort mit seiner Umgebung im Hintergrund.
Wenn Sie vom Hügel Richtung Norden schauen, sehen Sie unten im Tal Ziegenställe. Jenseits der Ställe befindet sich ein Bergkamm, der das Tal umringt. Das ist Ihr nächstes Ziel. Folgen Sie auf den Ziegenpfaden den Hang hinunter zu den Ziegenställen (die beste Strecke ist mit roten und weißen Streifen an den Büschen oder roter Farbe auf Steinen gekennzeichnet). Nach 500m überqueren Sie ein kleines Rinnsaal und kommen bei den Ställen an. Gehen Sie auf dem Feldweg an den Ställen vorbei Richtung Osten, bis Sie eine kleine Felsspitze erreichen, die auf einen Bach herunterblickt. Auf der anderen Seite des Baches stehen zwei Olivenbäume, die den Pfad zum Hügel andeuten. Überqueren Sie den Bach und steigen Sie auf dem steilen Pfad Richtung Osten, dann nach Westen, und in 50m Höhe kommen Sie an einem alten Olivenhain an. Der Pfad geht durch den Hain hindurch auf eine große Felswand zu.

The author admiring the view from the ridge above Sikia.
Der Autor bewundert die Aussicht auf die Gebirgshöhe bei Sikia

Guenther meets a Greek goatherder on the Sikia walk.
Günther trifft einen Ziegenhirten auf dem Weg nach Sikia

small grove, then swings east towards a large rock face. Pass directly below and round to the right of the very large rock to arrive at a large field. Follow the left hand edge of the field past a large, weather carved rock to reach a second summit; at approximately 280m above sea level. This is another fine viewpoint.

Now follow the good rocky track leading northwest along the ridge, which arrives at yet another high level field in a further 400m. Cross this field, passing a large rock to your left, and climb west towards a lone tree.

Continue on towards the ridge in front and, as the field is left behind, the ground drops away into the valley on your left. Continue round the head of the valley, gradually climbing in a northwesterly direction, and enjoy the fine

Gehen Sie an der Wand vorbei, rechts um einen sehr großen Stein herum, bis Sie auf ein großes Feld kommen. Gehen Sie am linken Feldrand und an einem großen, zerklüfteten Fels vorbei zu der zweiten Spitze, ca. 280m über dem Meeresspiegel. Hier befindet sich ein weiterer Aussichtspunkt.

Folgen Sie nun dem Bergpfad Richtung Nordwesten auf dem Bergrücken entlang, bis Sie eine weitere Kuppe, 400m weiter erreichen. Gehen Sie über das Feld, an einem großen Felsen zu Ihrer linken vorbei, und wandern Sie Richtung Westen auf einen einzelstehenden Baum zu. Gehen Sie weiter auf den Hang zu, bis Sie das Feld verlassen haben und der Pfad nach links hinunter ins Tal führt. Gehen Sie am Rande des Tals geradeaus, in nordwestliche

views in all directions. As you continue a grassy ridge appears ahead and to your right. Make for this ridge to see over into the next valley. A large inclined rock, shaped like a lizard's head, with a small grassy area to the right, is seen next. Climb up to this rock for magnificent views of the sea to the east and the valley that lies beneath us. This rock at 345m is the highest point on the route.

Continue west, descending to a field about 70m away, then turn left into another field 40m to the south. Here turn right, descending to the bottom of a small dip and rising up the other side.

At the edge of the field continue on along the goat track to the neck of the valley, cross the stream and climb straight up the other side. Here a maze of goat tracks head south as they traverse around the corner, to the left of a very large rock, in order to access the next small field.

The best track should be marked with red paint on the rocks and plastic tape on the bushes. Skirt round the top of the field to exit by a path at the top right hand corner. This leads up to a small col, which is crossed to continue southwest around the head of the valley, providing superb views to the east.

The track now descends gradually for about 300m, before rising on an excellent path to the top of the next col. From here descend towards the goat pens in the valley below for 150m or so, when a field appears to the left. Cross the top of this field to arrive at another field containing beehives.

Directly ahead, across the second field, is a dirt track,

Richtung und genießen Sie Ausblicke in alle Himmelsrichtungen. Unterwegs treffen Sie auf einen grasigen Bergrücken, der rechts zu sehen ist. Gehen Sie auf diesem Bergrücken entlang, während Sie ins nächste Tal hinunterschauen können. Als nächstes sehen Sie einen großen, gekrümmten Felsen, der die Form eines Echsenkopfes hat, mit einem Feld zu Ihrer Rechten. Klettern Sie auf den Felsen und schauen Sie aus 345m Höhe - das ist der höchste Punkt der Wanderung - nach Osten, auf das Meer und das unter Ihnen liegende Tal.

Gehen Sie Richtung Westen, 70m weiter über ein Feld und biegen Sie nach weiteren 40m links auf ein anderes Feld Richtung Süden. Gehen Sie jetzt nach rechts und steigen Sie eine kleine Bergsenke ab und auf der anderen Seite wieder hinauf. Gehen Sie am Feldrand entlang auf einem Ziegenpfad zum Anfang des Tales, überqueren Sie einen Bach und steigen Sie auf der anderen Seite geradeaus weiter. Von hier aus geht ein Gewirr von Ziegenpfaden Richtung Süden, um einen sehr großen Felsen auf der linken Seite herum und auf das nächste Feld. Der beste Weg ist mit roter Farbe auf den Felsen gekennzeichnet. Gehen Sie um das Feld herum und an der oberen rechten Ecke weiter durch einen kleinen Pass hindurch Richtung Südwesten und am Rande des Tales entlang. Es bietet sich ein herrlicher Ausblick Richtung Osten. Jetzt geht es 300m geradlinig hinunter und auf einem deutlichen Pfad wieder hinauf zur nächsten Felsenge. Von hier gehen Sie ca. 150m hinunter auf die Ziegenställe

rising to the brow of the hill. Cross the field to reach the track at its highest point. The return route follows this track down to the southeast, and back towards Sikia.
After 700m of descent a track joins from the left. Turn right onto this track and continue down to pass a rock, which has been sculpted by the weather to look like a human face. A further 350m of steep descent bring us to a bigger road from the right. Turn left onto this road and continue down, to reach the old track leading back down to point **A** on the map. From here retrace your steps back down to the village and a welcoming taverna.

*Many years ago it was a common site to see the Charcoal burners at work in the forests of Europe. Today the only evidence of this once widespread occupation are the flat circular hearths,

zu. Gehen Sie erneut über ein Feld, das auf der linken Seite zu sehen ist, bis zu einem anderen Feld, auf dem Bienenstöcke stehen.
Direkt vor dem zweiten Feld führt ein Feldweg auf die Hügel zu. Gehen Sie über das Feld zu dieser Straße, aber hinunter Richtung Südosten, zurück nach Sikia. Nach 700m mündet von Ihrer linken Seite ein Pfad auf die Straße ein. Gehen Sie rechts auf diesem Weg an einem Felsen, der wie ein Gesicht geformt ist, vorbei. Nach weiteren 350m steilen Abstiegs überqueren Sie eine große, von rechts kommende Straße. Biegen Sie links auf diese Straße, bis Sie auf die alte Straße treffen, die zu Punkt **A** auf der Landkarte, zurückführt. Laufen Sie die letzten Schritte zurück ins Dorf und in eine der sehr einladenden Tavernen.

*Die Holzkohlengewinnung war vor vielen Jahren ein alltägliches Bild in den Wäldern

A weather carved rock in the shape of a lizard's head, seen towards the end of this walk.

Felsen in Form eines Echsen-Kopfes am Ende des Weges

where the fires were built, and the occasional stone built bread oven. However this ancient craft is still practised in Halkidiki.
Near Taxiarchis in the Holomondas mountains I came across wood stacked ready for converting to charcoal.
The fire is lit and then the burning is slowed right down by covering the stack with wet earth to reduce the oxygen supply. While burning the fire must be watched night and day to ensure a good yield of charcoal. When the fire breaks out at any point it must be quickly sealed in again with wet earth. After several days the fire goes out and the earth cover is removed to reveal a stack of lump wood charcoal.

Europas, damals war auch der Beruf des Köhlers noch weit verbreitet. Heute zeugen nur noch flache, runde Erhebungen von den Plätzen, an denen früher die Holzkohle gewonnen wurde und sich gelegentlich auch Steinöfen zum Backen von Brot befanden. Auf Chalkidiki gehört dieses Handwerk allerdings noch nicht der Vergangenheit an.
In der Nähe von Taxiarchis, im Holomondas Gebirge, habe ich solche abgedeckten Stapel von Holzscheitern entdeckt, aus denen Holzkohle hergestellt wird. Dabei wird der Stapel mit feuchter Erde abgedeckt und unter Luftabschluß bei schwacher Hitze gebrannt. Dieser Prozeß wird Tag und Nacht überwacht und immer wenn eine Flamme auflodert, wird sie sofort wieder mit feuchter Erde erstickt. Nach einigen Tagen erlischt das Feuer und die Holzkohlenstücke werden unter der Erdschicht ausgegraben.

A charcoal burner's stack in the woods near Taxiarchis

Ein Holzkohlescheiter in den Wäldern bei Taxiarchis

21700

The land
of
the living tradition

Athos

Die
unzugängliche
Halbinsel

Καφενειόν
Ο
Χαρίλαος

Ammouliani - Island Walk / Insel Wanderung

Amouliani Island lies off the eastern coast of the Athos peninsula at the northern end of the gulf of Agion Oros. It is inhabited and there is a regular ferryboat service between the island and Tripiti at the northern end of the peninsula. There is ample parking at Tripiti and one can cross as a foot passenger for a nominal amount (160 GRD or 32p in 1999).
The route is mainly an easy walk along unmade farm access roads with about 1km of more difficult scrub and tree covered hillside, in order to reach a fine clifftop viewpoint.
The time required is about 2 hours.

With a population of about 400, this is the only inhabited island on Halkidiki. There are traces of a settlement here since Classical Greek times. Later this group of islands became part of the lands of one of the Mt. Athos monasteries. After 1922 refugees from Asia Minor settled here. The people on the island are mainly fisherman or merchant seamen.

Die Insel Amouliani liegt an der Ostküste der Halbinsel Athos im Norden des Golfs von Agion Oros. Zu der bewohnten Insel gibt es einen regelmäßigen Fahrverkehr von Tripiti aus, im Norden der Halbinsel Athos. Es gibt genügend Parkplätze in Tripiti und die Überfahrt für Fußgänger ist nicht teuer (160 GRD/ ungefähr 1 DM pro Person, Stand 1999).
Die Route ist eine leichte Wanderung auf Feldwegen, die zu Bauernhöfen führen. Um auf einen der höchsten, felsigen Punkte der Insel zu gelangen, folgen Sie ca. 1km Ziegenpfaden die durch Gebüsch und dichten Bewuchs führen.
Dauer: ca. 2 Stunden

Mit ungefähr 400 Einwohnern ist Amouliani die einzige bewohnte Insel von Chalkidiki. Es gibt verschiedene Reste von Ansiedlungen, die aus der Antike stammen. Später gehörte diese Inselgruppe zu einer der Länderreien eines Athosklosters. Nach 1922 wurde die Insel von Flüchtlingen aus Kleinasien besiedelt. Die Bevölkerung besteht hauptsächlich aus Fischern und Matrosen, die auf Handelsschiffen arbeiten.

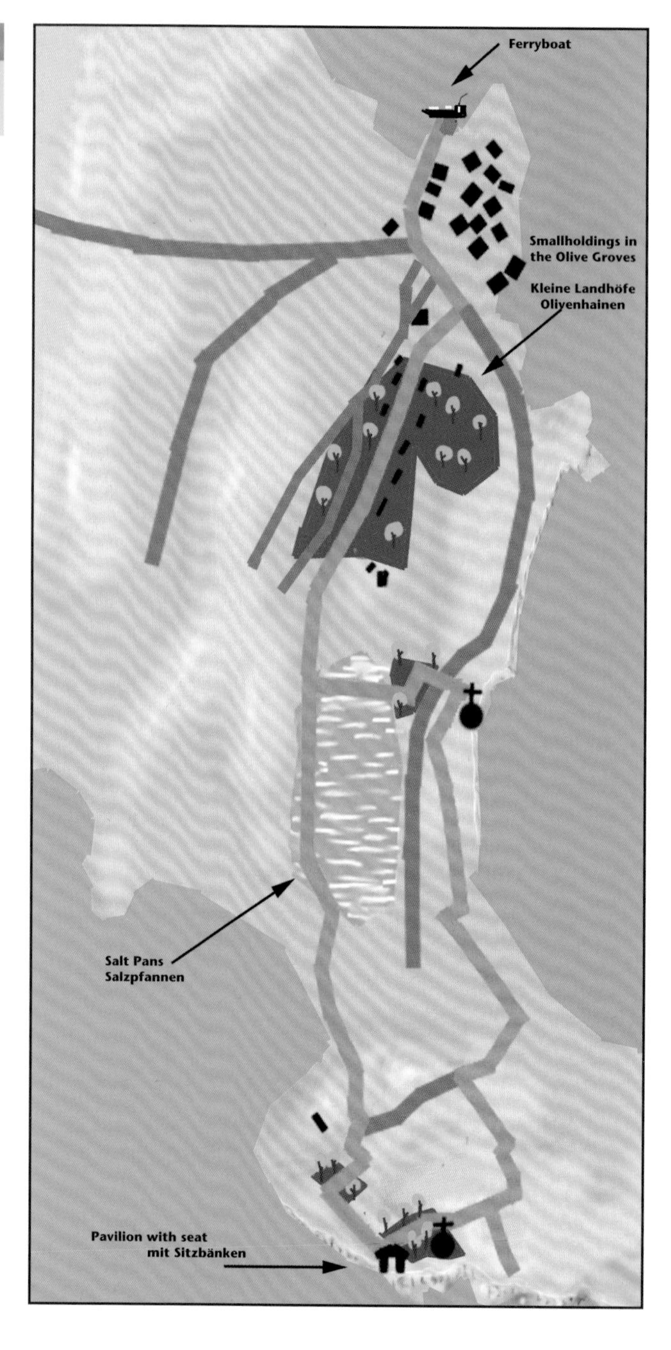
Ferryboat
Smallholdings in
the Olive Groves
Kleine Landhöfe
Olivenhainen
Salt Pans
Salzpfannen
Pavilion with seat
mit Sitzbänken

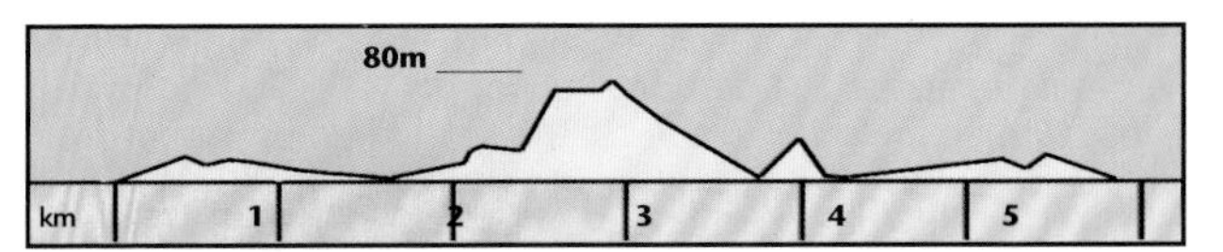

The waymarker that points south up the main street of the village. In 150m or so a supermarket is passed as the street curves round to the southeast. 250m further on look for a *Mega* supermarket on the right. Turn right here and follow the street that leads southwest, past a brightly painted primary school. In 300m or so the road becomes a track and passes through a builders yard containing stockpiles of various building materials. In the next 500m or so the track passes through a variety of smallholdings with chickens, turkeys, pigs, goats etc. running free amongst the olives or housed in ramshackle pens. Eventually the track arrives at a large but shallow salt-water lake, previously used to obtain salt by evaporation of seawater (salt pans), and runs along its perimeter. At the end of the lake the path goes over a small rise to arrive at a junction. Turn left here and follow the track; which leads towards the hill directly in front. The sea is over to the right. Follow the track up the hill to reach a group of buildings standing prominently on the hillside, but don't forget to look back and enjoy the marvellous view to the rear. Continue past the houses on your right as the track descends the other side of the rise to arrive in 50m or so at a point where a small track leads off to the left and upwards. Here you can make a decision. If your footwear is

Sobald Sie die Fähre verlassen haben, folgen Sie der Hauptstraße, die Richtung Süden die in das Dorf hineinführt. Nach 150m führt die Straße an einem Supermarkt vorbei nach Südosten. Nach 250m sehen Sie zu Ihrer Rechten einen Supermarkt namens Mega. Hier biegen Sie rechts ab und kommen auf eine Straße Richtung Südwesten, vorbei an einer hell gestrichenen Volksschule. Nach 300m wechselt die Straße zu einem Pfad über und führt durch ein Werksgelände, auf dem Baumaterial gelagert wird. Auf den folgenden 500m gehen Sie an verschiedenen kleinen Landbesitzen mit Hühnern, Puten, Schweinen, Ziegen usw. vorbei, die unter den Olivenbäumen umherlaufen oder in reparaturbedürftigen Ställen gehalten werden. Schließlich kommt der Pfad an einen großen, aber flachen Salzwasserteich, wo früher durch Meerwasserverdampfung Salz gewonnen wurde (Salzpfanne). Der Weg führt um den Teich herum und folgt am Ende einem Weg hinauf zu einer Kreuzung. Biegen Sie links ab und gehen Sie auf dem Pfad geradeaus weiter bergauf. Das Meer befindet sich zu Ihrer rechten Seite. Oben auf dem Hügel angelangt erblicken Sie eine Reihe von Gebäuden, die am Hang stehen, aber drehen Sie sich ruhig um und genießen Sie die Aussicht. Gehen Sie an den Häusern zu Ihrer Rechten vorbei und steigen Sie auf

adequate for climbing up a wooded hillside then continue on down the track. If not then you can take this left turn and it will rejoin the route later, but will avoid the climb to the viewpoint mentioned in the introduction to the walk (see the map).
The route now crosses a stream by a ford and curves west to climb the hill. In 200m the sandy road bears left and ascends to an open area with a wooden pavilion, table and chairs, perched on the edge of the cliff. This is a good place for refreshment and to enjoy the view, but a more spectacular viewpoint awaits us ahead. Suitably refreshed cross the road into the olive grove (look for the waymarker) and walk east, looking for a small white church, about 100m into the grove on the right side. The path passes to the left of the church over an old drystone wall and threads its way through the undergrowth, over another wall, to reach a more open area and a path junction in another 100m. The main route continues straight on, but it is well worth turning right here to follow the goat track that leads to the prominent rockface about 50m to the right. From here there are beautiful views of the island and coast in most directions. Returning from this viewpoint to the path junction, continue northeast for a further 50m (look for red markers on the stones) to arrive at a stony outcrop. Carefully descend from here onto the old track a few metres below, which contours down the hillside and curves

dem Weg den Hang wieder ab, bis Sie nach 50m an einem Punkt angelangen, wo ein anderer Weg links bergauf führt. Hier haben Sie die Wahl: Wenn Ihre Schuhe gutes Profil aufweisen, können Sie auf dem direkten Weg den Waldhang aufsteigen. Wenn Sie aber nicht zu dem Aussichtspunkt, der in der Einleitung erwähnt wurde, hinaufsteigen wollen, dann biegen Sie auf den linken Pfad ab. Er schließt sich später wieder der Hauptroute an (siehe Landkarte).
Der Weg überquert jetzt durch eine Furt einen kleinen Bach und geht nach Westen hoch. Nach 200m biegt der Weg nach links und steigt zu einer Lichtung auf, wo ein Pavillon, Tisch und Stühle aus Holz am Rande der Klippen stehen. Ein geigneter Ort für eine Erfrischungspause, mit einem schönen Ausblick, aber ein noch schönerer erwartet Sie etwas später. Nach der Pause gehen Sie die Straße, die in einen Olivenhain führt (siehe Wegweiser), Richtung Osten und nach 100m sehen Sie eine, kleine weiße Kapelle, rechts im Hain stehen. Der Weg führt links an der Kapelle vorbei, über eine alte Bruchsteinmauer und durch das Gestrüpp hindurch über eine andere Mauer bis zu einer Gabelung auf offenem Land. Die Hauptroute geht geradeaus weiter, aber es lohnt sich, hier rechts abzubiegen und auf einem Ziegenpfad zu der Felswand in 50m Höhe zu steigen. Von hier oben haben Sie herrliche Aussicht in fast alle Richtungen, über die Insel und die Küste. Kehren Sie von dem Aussichtspunkt wieder zurück zu der Weggabelung

right to keep to the ridge. To the left a broad scrub and rock covered slope descends to a small stone outcrop, which is just above another track, leading to the beach. Look for the red marks on the rocks and descend this slope to the north, whilst enjoying the panoramic view in front of the north end of the island. At the bottom of the slope turn right onto the track, which is the continuation of the route suggested as a bypass for this difficult section. On reaching the beach turn left onto the unsurfaced road and continue north. The road bears right as it climbs a slope with an ekliassis at its highest point. It then swings left to meet a tarmac road. Cross the road diagonally and turn left down a track to black gates. Just before the gates turn right into the olive grove (look for the waymarker signs). Cross the grove to emerge onto the salt pans seen on the outward journey. Cross the northern edge of the salt lake to rejoin the outward route and retrace your steps, past all the farm animals, to the ferry.

Amouliani Island
TraditionalTransport
Traditionelles Vekehrsmittel

und gehen Sie weiter Richtung Norden, wo Sie nach 50m auf eine steinige Felsnase stoßen (schauen Sie nach roten Markierungen auf den Steinen). Steigen Sie vorsichtig auf dem alten Pfad, der ein paar Meter tiefer liegt, abwärts und halten Sie sich immer rechts am Hang entlang. Auf der linken Seite führt ein breiter mit Gebüsch und Gestein bedeckter Hang zu einer kleinen Felsnase, die direkt über einem anderen Pfad liegt, der zum Strand führt. Schauen Sie nach den roten Markierungen auf den Felsen und steigen Sie den Hang Richtung Norden hinunter. Genießen Sie den Panoramablick auf das Nordende der Insel! Am Ende des Hangs biegen Sie rechts ab. Jetzt befinden Sie sich auf dem Pfad, der diese schwierige Wegstrecke umgangen hat. Am Strand angelangt biegen Sie links auf die ungeteerte Straße Richtung Norden ab. Die Straße dreht nach rechts ab und steigt einen Hang hinauf. Oben auf dem höchsten Punkt steht ein *Eklissaki*. Dann geht es nach links auf eine Asphaltstraße. Überqueren Sie diagonal die Straße und gehen Sie links auf einem Pfad bis zum schwarzen Tor. Kurz vor dem Tor biegen Sie rechts in den Olivenhain ab (siehe Wegmarkierungen). Nach dem Olivenhain erscheinen wieder die Salz-pfannen vom Anfang der Route. Gehen Sie am nordlichen Rand des Salz-wasserteichs vorbei, um wieder auf die Ausgangsroute zu kommen, und von hier gehen Sie wieder den gleichen Weg, vorbei an den Ställen zurück zum Fähr-anleger.

Ouranoupolis - Mt. Athos Border Grenze

This easy route takes one from the village of Ouranopolis along a path which follows the coast to the border of Athos. It then turns north along the border fence for a few hundred yards, before turning west to ascend a forest track. This track gradually climbs the wooded hillside overlooking the coastline between Ouranopolis and the Athos Border, as it meanders round the side of the valley. The route provides good forest walking with fine views of the vineyards and olive groves in this sheltered valley, as well as the coast beyond.

(2 hours)

Diese Wanderung führt von Ouranoupolis über einen Pfad zur Grenze der Mönchsrepublik Athos. Dann verläuft sie Richtung Norden, einige hundert Meter entlag der Grenzlinie, bis sie Richtung Westen auf einen Forstweg abzweigt. Dieser Pfad steigt geradlinig den bewaldeten Berghang hinauf. Von hier kann man die ganze Küstenlinie zwischen Ouranoupolis und der Grenze zu Athos überblicken. Die Route führt durch schöne, lichte Waldstücke mit herrlichen Ausblicken auf die Weinberge und die Olivenhaine, die sich an diesem geschützten Hang befinden, sowie auf die gesamte Küste im Hintergrund.

Dauer : 2 Stunden

Athos is a self-administered part of the Greek State. The monks established their monasteries there in the 9th century and it is the records they kept which have provided most of the historical information from that date onwards. The tower of Prosphorion in Ouronopolis is the biggest and best preserved tower in Halkidiki and dates back to the 14th century. It was damaged by an earthquake in the 19th century and was subsequently repaired. The present roof dates back to that period.

Athos ist eine vom griechischen Staat unabhängige Region, die sich selbst verwaltet. Im 9. Jahrhundert gründeten dort die Mönche ihre Klöster und aus den schriftlichen Aufzeichnungen, die sie seitdem führten, gewann man wichtige Informationen über die Geschichte der Region. Der Turm von Prophoriou in Ouranoupolis ist der besterhaltenste Turm auf Chalkidiki und wird auf das 14. Jahrhundert zurückdatiert. Er wurde bei einem Erdbeben im 19. Jahrhundert zerstört, aber kurz darauf wieder aufgebaut. Das heutige Dach des Turmes stammt noch aus jener Zeit.

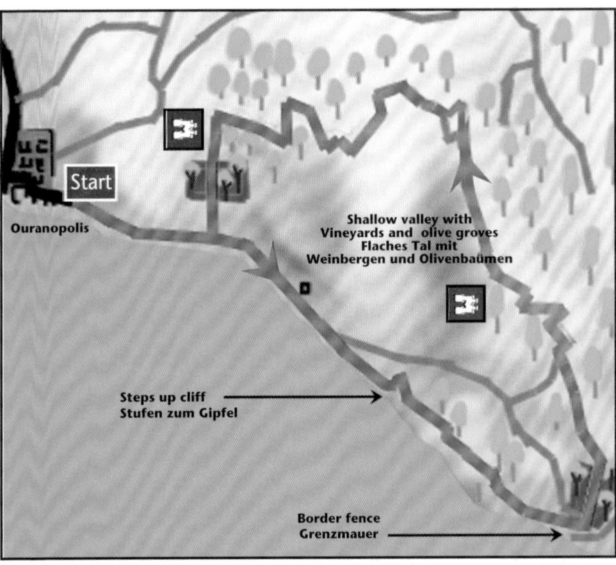

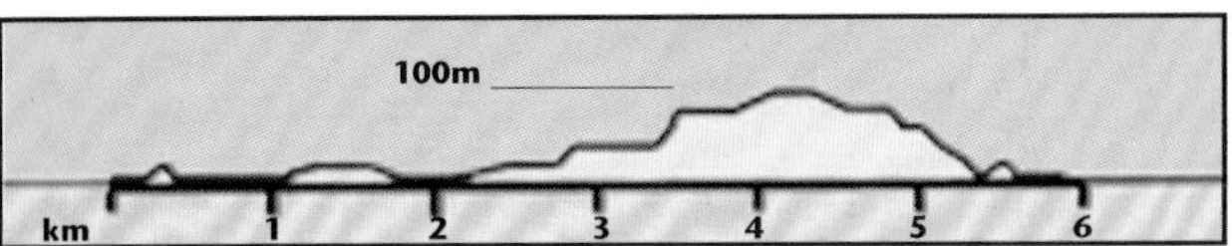

This walk begins at the seafront in Ouranopolis. Turn left at the tower of Prosphorion to arrive in a short distance at a wide unmade road with ample parking space. From here walk on along the road with the sea on the right. The road diverts to the left around a building then narrows and climbs a small hill. A small road to the left here is the one we will return on at the end of the walk. Continue on along the track, which turns to the southeast, following the shoreline, to a point where the track turns away from the sea. The route now continues along the beach (look for the waymarker) towards a point where a large outcrop of rocks protudes into the sea. About 100 m before

Die Wanderung beginnt am Strand von Ouranoupolis. Gehen Sie am Prophoriou Turm links vorbei, bis Sie zu einer großen, halbfertigen Straße mit ausreichend Platz zum Parken kommen. Von hier wandern Sie immer am Meer entlang. Die Straße biegt nach links ab, um ein Gebäude herum, und wird schmaler, je höher Sie den kleinen Hügel aufsteigen. Auf der linken Seite sehen Sie eine kleine Straße, auf der Sie am Ende der Wanderung zurückkehren werden.

Wandern Sie weiter auf der Straße, die an der Küste entlang Richtung Südosten führt, sich aber dann später vom Strand entfernt. Hier führt unser Weg direkt am Strand weiter (schauen Sie nach den Wegweisern) auf

these rocks the path climbs to the top of the steep cliff on the left, via steps which zig zag up the hillside. The path continues to follow the coast through the brush and woodland on the clifftop for a distance of 700m and then descends through bushes to the beach at the Athos Border. Here at the end of the track stand the ruins of *Frangokastro* castle, which dates back to at least the 11th century, as well as the border fence and its police office. In addition there is a nice section of beach, marred only by the concrete wall that juts out into the sea.

Notices here inform people that no access is allowed, except with the appropriate visa, * **and no access under any circumstances to women.**

To continue the walk follow the track through the olive grove, which leads past the ruined castle to join a woodland track going north. This fine path meanders gradually upwards through shady trees, constrained on one side by a forested hillside and on the other by a deep ravine, which provides an effectual natural barrier to Athos. However in a distance of 400m our route turns left up a narrow valley through an old olive grove in order to ascend a fine mountain track that twists and turns, following the contours of the hillside, as it gradually climbs back through open woodland, towards Ouranoupolis. The path provides fine views of the cultivated valley below, with the coast beyond. Eventually the path completes its traverse round the valley and turns back towards the sea. Here it

eine Felsnase zu, die in die See hinausragt. Ungefähr 100m vor diesem Felsen steigt der Pfad in Serpentinen mit Stufen die steilen Klippen hinauf. Dieser Pfad geht ca. 700m auf dem Rücken entlang, durch das Gebüsch und den Wald, und fällt dann wieder zum Strand an der Athosgrenze ab. Hier treffen Sie auf die Ruine der *Frangokastro*-Burg, die aus dem 11. Jahrhundert stammt. Hier befindet sich auch der Grenzübergang und die Polizeiwache. Übrigens ist dieser Strand sehr schön, abgesehen von der Betonwand der Grenzbefestigung, die ins Wasser ragt. Warnschilder weisen darauf hin, daß der Zutritt nur mit gültigem Visum* erlaubt ist, und daß der **Eintritt für Frauen strengstens verboten ist.**

Weiter geht es auf dem Pfad durch den Olivenhain, an der Burgruine vorbei und auf einem anderen Weg Richtung Norden. Dieser Weg leitet Sie geradeaus hinauf, durch die schattigen Bäume hindurch, eingezwängt zwischen dem Waldhang auf der einen Seite und einer tiefen Schlucht auf der anderen Seite, die eine natürliche Grenze zu Athos bildet. Nach 400m zweigt der Weg nach links ab und führt Sie durch ein schmales Tal und einen alten Olivenhain, bis Sie einen schönen Bergweg erreichen. Wandern Sie auf diesem Weg durch den Wald bequem den Hang entlang in Richtung Ouranoupolis. Werfen Sie einen Blick auf das Anbaugebiet unten im Tal und die Strände im Hintergrund. Der Weg führt schließlich um das Tal herum

passes through a shady pinewood to reveal, at the next turn, a fine view over the town and coast. The path now descends quite steeply to the coast with olive groves gardens, chickens, turkeys etc. on both sides to add colour and noise to the rural setting. The track emerges on the outward coastal path to the border about 500m from the start. Turn right to return to the town centre with its Tavernas and shops.

* The conditions for non-Greeks to obtain visas are very strict and numbers are restricted to about 10 persons per day.

und kehrt dann zum Meer zurück. Sie gehen durch einen schattigen Kiefernwald, und an der nächsten Kurve erblicken Sie wieder den Ort und den Strand unter sich. Die Forststraße führt jetzt steil bergab zum Meer. Auf beiden Seiten befinden sich Olivenhaine und Gärten mit Hühnerställen. Die Forststraße bringt Sie wieder auf den Weg zur Athosgrenze, den Sie bereits kennen, ca. 500m vom Ausgangspunkt entfernt. Biegen Sie nach rechts und kehren Sie ins Ortszentrum mit seinen Tavernen und Geschäften zurück.

* Für ausländische Besucher ist es relativ schwierig, ein Einreisevisum zu erhalten. Außerdem ist die Besucherzahl auf zehn Ausländer pro Tag beschränkt.

Left: The Tower of Ouranoupolis

Links: Der Turm von Ouranoupolis

Mt. Athos Border
Berg Athos Grenze

Ouranoupolis Hotels

This walk links the three hotels Alexandros, Eagles Palace and Hotel Aristoteles, which lie along the road between Tripiti and Ouranoupolis. The walk uses the high ground behind the hotels as a platform for viewing the Gulf of Agion Oros, the Island of Amouliani and the hills of Sithonia beyond. From points along the route, the opposite side of the peninsula and the gulf of Ierissos can be seen.

The high ground can be accessed directly from all three hotels, or from Ouranoupolis, so it is possible to arrange a walk between one hotel and another, or from an hotel to Ouranoupolis, and then return along the road, by bus or taxi as required.

Diese Wanderung verbindet die drei Hotels Alexandros, Eagles Palace und Hotel Aristoteles miteinander, die alle an der Straße zwischen Tripiti und Ouranoupolis liegen. Der Höhenzug hinter den Hotels ist ein idealer Aussichtsbalkon auf den Golf von Agion Oros, die Insel Amouliani und die Berge von Sithonia jenseits des Golfs. Von vielen Stellen der Wanderung bieten sich auch gute Ausblicke auf die andere Seite der Halbinsel Athos und den Golf von Ierissos.

Der Höhenzug ist von allen drei Hotels aus leicht besteigbar, und ebenfalls von Ouranoupolis aus, so daß Sie diese Wanderung zwischen zwei Hotels, oder von einem der Hotel aus nach Ouranoupolis durchführen können, und dann mit Taxi oder Bus auf der Straße zurückkehren.

The route is described from Ouranoupolis
(Point **A** on the map).
This is a steep ascent up a farm access road onto the plateau 100m above. The surrounding terrain during the ascent is mainly gorse and scrub, which can be a blaze of colour in the Springtime. Look for the waymarker indicating the start of the route and follow the road up

Die Beschreibung der Route geht von Ouranoupolis aus (Punkt **A** auf der Landkarte).
Sie beginnt mit einem steilen Aufstieg auf einem Feldweg zum über Ouranoupolis gelegenen Höhenzug in 100m Höhe. Während des Aufstiegs sind Sie umgeben von Büschen und Stechginstersträuchern, die besonders im Frühling eine Farbenpracht darstellen.

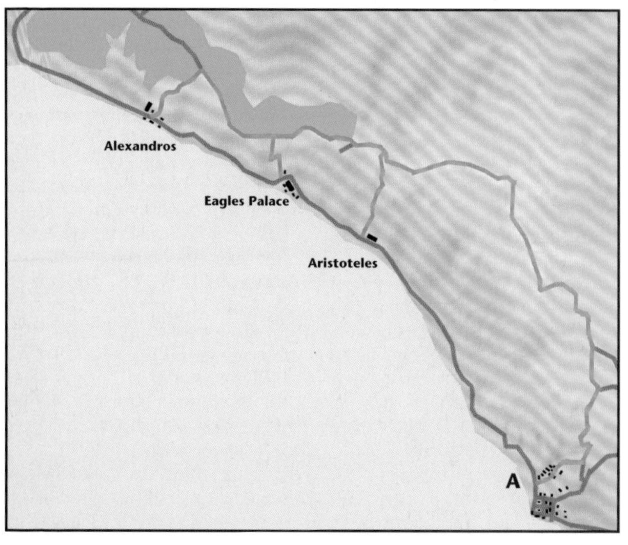

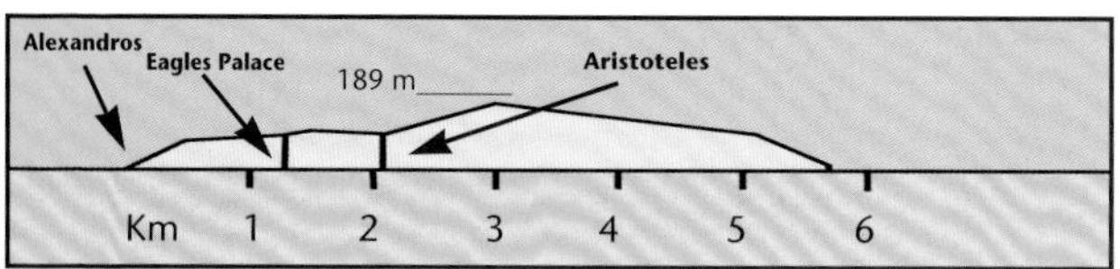

and out of the village in a northeasterly direction. At minor junctions the route keeps to the left, continuing to climb and swinging round towards the north as it does so. About 600m from the start a right fork is taken. Look for the waymarker to confirm the correct route. The route climbs up through gorse and scrub to level out about 2km from the start. Soon the gorse and scrub is left behind, to be replaced with fields and woodland. From here good views can be obtained to the northwest of Amouliani Island, its satellite islets and the gulf beyond. A few hundred metres further on, about 3km from the start, a high point is reached and it is possible to see across to Ierissos Bay, on the easterly

Schauen Sie nach dem Wegweiser, der den Start der Route anzeigt, und folgen Sie der Straße aus dem Ort heraus in nordöstliche Richtung. Bei den Abzweigungen halten Sie sich immer links aufwärts, Richtung Norden. Nach 600m folgen Sie dem Weg der nach rechts führt. Achten Sie auf den Wegweiser! Die Route führt ca. 2km hinauf, durch die Sträucher und das Gebüsch, bis sie auf flacheres Gelände führt. Sie befinden sich jetzt zwischen Feldern und einem Wald. Von hier haben Sie gute Sicht über den nordwestlichen Teil der Insel Amouliani, ihren kleinen vorgelagerten Inselchen und den Golf dahinter. Ein paar hundert Meter weiter, ca. 3km vom Startpunkt entfernt, erreichen Sie einen weiteren Hügel, von dem Sie gute Sicht

coast of this narrow peninsula. The track now turns to the northwest and and gradually descends to a junction. Here a waymarker should indicate the route down to the Hotel Aristoteles. The track along the plateau continues northwest, climbing slightly as it passes through wheatfields to reach another high point. From here a slight descent to the east leads to another junction (about 800m from the path down to Hotel Aristoteles), where a waymarker should indicate the way down to the Hotel Eagles Palace. On a clear day the views across the gulf from here can be excellent. The track continues across more cultivated fields, turning away from the coast, but still gradually descending to arrive at another junction about 1km beyond the Eagles Palace junction. Turn left here down the hill to arrive at the Hotel Alexandros in a further 400m.

bis zur Ierissos Bucht haben, die an der Ostküste dieser schmalen Halbinsel liegt. Der Pfad dreht jetzt nach Nordwesten ab und fällt zu einer Gabelung ab. Ein Wegweiser müßte Ihnen den Weg hinunter zum Hotel Aristoteles andeuten. Der Pfad geht auf dem Höhenrücken weiter Richtung Nordwesten und steigt leicht an, vorbei an Weizenfeldern, bis zu einem weiteren Hügel. Von hier führt ein kurzer Abstieg ostwärts zu einer weiteren Gabelung (etwa 800m) entfernt von der Abzweigung zum Hotel Aristoteles, wo ein Wegweiser den Weg zum Hotel Eagles Palace anzeigt. An klaren Tagen ist die Aussicht auf den Golf atemberaubend! Der Pfad führt weiter an Weizenfeldern vorbei. Sie ereichen eine weitere Abzweigung. Biegen Sie links ab und steigen Sie den Berg 400m abwärts bis zum Hotel Alexandros.

Boat building the traditional way

Traditionelle Schiffswerft

Eklissaki in Nea Roda

Polygiros - Tsoukalas - Polygiros

This walk takes one up onto the mountain overlooking Polygiros from the southeast. The first part of the trip provides panoramic views of the city and terrain to the northwest, as it winds its way up to the church of the *Prophet Elias*. This church, with its large stone cross, is a prominent landmark that stands high above the town. The route then follows the mountain ridge leading east to the Telecommunications masts on the summit of Stavrou Tuba (942m). This is followed by a steep descent down a ridge back to Polygiros. The paths on this route have all been made through the scrubland in the last few years and should be in good condition, so stout shoes should suffice (2 1/2 hours).

This hillside, previously inaccessible, is well endowed with flowering shrubs, flowers and butterflies, according to the season.

Polygiros, standing at 600m above sea level, is the administrative centre of Halkidiki. Inhabited since prehistoric times, the citizens of

Diese Wanderung führt sie hinauf auf den Berg oberhalb Polygiros, südöstlich der Stadt. Auf der ersten Etappe der Wanderung bieten sich Panoramablicke über die Stadt und die Umgebung im Nordwesten, bis Sie oben an der Kirche Profitis Ilias angelangt sind. Diese Kirche mit ihrem großen steinernen Kreuz, ist ein bekanntes Wahrzeichen, das die Stadt überragt. Dann führt der Wanderweg weiter den Kamm entlang Richtung Osten, zu den Fernmeldemasten auf dem Gipfel von Stavrou Tuba (942m). Daraufhin geht es durch eine Schlucht steil bergab zurück nach Polygiros. Die Wege wurden alle kürzlich vom Gestrüpp befreit und sind sehr gepflegt, so daß etwas festere Schuhe für diese Route ausreichend sind (Dauer: 2 1/2 Stunden).

Dieser Berghang, der bis vor kurzem vollkommen unzugänglich war, ist je nach Jahreszeit bedeckt mit blühenden Büschen, Blumen und Schmetterlingen.

Polygiros liegt 600m über dem Meeresspiegel und ist die Hauptstadt von Chalkidiki. Die Geschichte dieser Stadt reicht viele

Polygiros began the uprising in 1821 against the Turks. This eventually led to the ousting of the Turks from the area in 1912. Polygiros has an interesting archeological museum with artefacts from all over Halkidiki.

Jahrtausende zurück. 1821 ging von hier der Aufstand gegen die türkischen Besatzer und vertrieb diese 1912 schließlich ganz aus der Region. In Polygiros gibt es ein interessantes Archaeologisches Museum mit Kunstschaetzen aus ganz Chalkidiki.

The walk begins at a small pavilion and garden situated about 200m west, along the road from the hospital in Polygiros. A red brick built *Eklissaki* stands nearby. The town council constructed the path from here to the church of the *Prophet Elias*, and on to the summit of Stavrou

Ausgangspunkt der Wanderung ist ein kleiner Pavillon in einem Garten, 200m westlich der Straße, die zum Krankenhaus führt. Daneben steht ein kleines *Eklissaki* aus roten Backsteinen. Vor einigen Jahren ließ der Stadtrat einen Weg zur Profitis Ilias Kirche und zu der Gipfelspitze von Stavrou

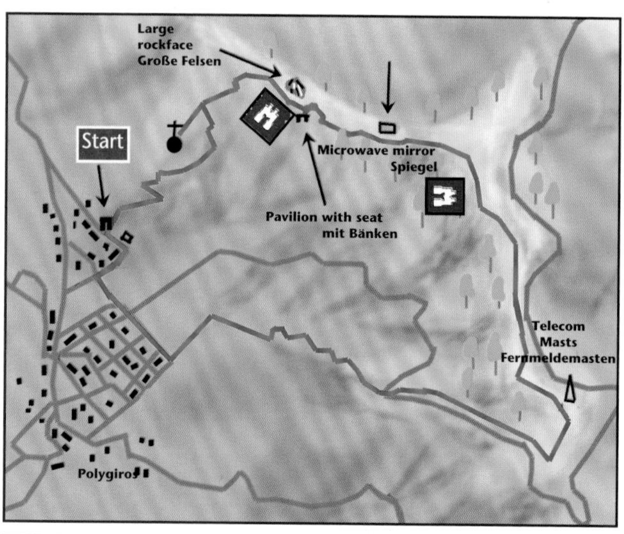

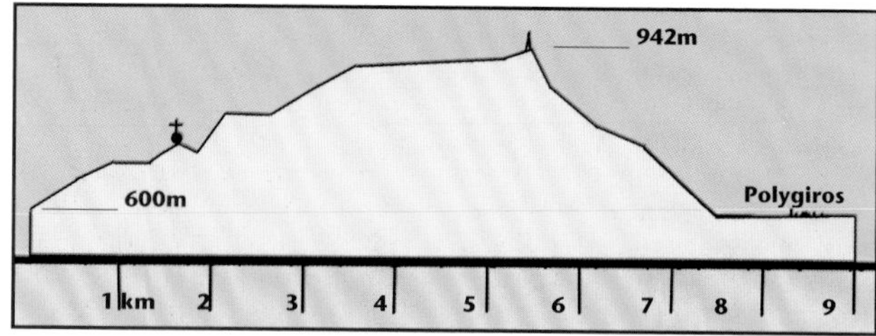

Tuba, some years ago. the route winds through the dense vegetation on the hillside, providing frequent panoramic views over the city and valley below, with Mount Olympus on the horizon beyond; more than 60km away. The path emerges onto the access road to the church about 200m from it. Spare time here to go up to the church and enjoy the fine view over the town from this elevated position. Retrace your steps to the junction below the church to continue the walk. Here another recently constructed path leads eastwards, up onto the ridge towards the telecommunications masts. Wooden signposts in Greek indicate the distance as 1892m. The path is also marked with Poseidon signs. This track gradually climbs towards the ridge, meandering up and down as it follows the twists and turns in the hillside. In 500m the path passes below a large rockface to arrive at a viewpoint with shelter and bench seat in a further 300m. From here the track soon reaches the top of the ridge and passes through open woodland with rocky promontories overlooking the valley below, to arrive at a fenced children's park and picnic area.

The large rectangular metal construction is a microwave mirror, relaying the signal from a transmitter somewhere in the valley below to a receiver at another location.

The walk now continues eastwards along the ridge, which then swings to the south to approach the transmitting masts, which are placed at the highest point on the hillside. Follow the

Tuba errichten. Die Route fürt in Serpentinen durch dichte Vegetation des Berghangs, mit häufigen Panoramablicken über die Stadt und das Tal darunter, sogar der Olymp ist 60km entfernt am Horizont zu sehen. Der Weg erreicht die Zufahrtstraße zur Profitis Ilias Kirche ca. 200m vor der Kirche. Nehmen Sie sich Zeit und steigen Sie hinauf zu der Kirche. Genießen Sie den Ausblick aus dieser Höhe auf die Stadt. Gehen Sie zurück zu der Gabelung unterhalb der Kirche und folgen Sie dem neulich konstruierten Pfad ostwärts den Hang hinauf, zu den Fernmeldemasten. An einem Holzpfosten ist auf Griechisch die Entfernung (1892 m) angegeben. Es gibt aber auch die gewohnten Markierungsschilder. Der Pfad durchquert den Hang in Richtung der auffälligen Felsen. Nach 500m kommen Sie unterhalb der großen Felswand vorbei, und nach weiteren 300m zu einem Aussichtspunkt mit einer Hütte und Sitzbänken. Durch das Waldgebiet hindurch kommen Sie bald auf dem Kamm an. Von hier erreichen Sie bequem den höchsten Punkt, auf dem Sie einen umzäunten Kinderspielplatz und eine Picknickwiese finden.

Die große, rechteckige Metallkonstruktion ist ein Radiowellen-Spiegel, der ein Signal von einem Sender aus dem Tal zu einem Empfänger an einem anderen Ort überträgt.

Die Wanderung folgt jetzt ostwärts den Bergrücken entlang und dreht später nach Süden, wo Sie zu den Fernmeldemasten kommen die auf dem höchsten Punkt errichtet wurden. Folgen Sie den Poseidon - Wegweisern, die diesen neuen Weg duch das

Poseidon signs on this new route, cut through the dense vegetation. The path now descends down the steep ridge south of the summit to the east of Polygiros. Just above the asphalt road the track turns to travel parallel the road, giving fine views to the west, with Polygiros in the foreground.
Eventually the road is crossed as it swings northwards to contour the hillside and the path zig zags down a wide firebreak, cut along the line of the ridge leading back to Polygiros. A short walk through this developing area of the town will bring you back to the startpoint.

dichte Gebüsch anzeigen. Es geht jetzt den steilen Abhang südwärts des Gipfels hinunter zu der Ostseite von Polygiros. Kurz vor der Asphaltstraße biegt der Pfad ab und führt jetzt parallel zu der Asphaltstraße Richtung Westen. Von hier blicken Sie in steilem Winkel auf das direkt unter Ihnen gelegene Polygiros.
Schließich überqueren Sie die Asphaltstraße und gehen nordwärts an dem Berghang entlang. Der Pfad führt in Serpentinen über eine breite Feuerschneise, die am Hang nach unten führt, und endet in den Ausläufern von Polygiros. Ein kurzer Spaziergang durch die ständig wachsende Stadt bringt Sie schließlich zurück zum Ausgangspunkt.

Mt. Olympus can be seen in the distance in this view from the path, taken in January

Der Olymp im Hintergrund Die Aufnahme entstand im Januar

Taxiarchis - Vrastama

This walk between the mountain villages of Taxiarchis and Vrastama starts at a height of 640m above sea level and finishes at 450m, so it is mainly downhill with a few ups and downs along the way.

Diese Wanderung zwischen den Bergdörfern Taxiarchis und Vrastama beginnt in einer Höhe von 640m über dem Meeresspiegel und endet in einer Höhe von 450m über dem Meeresspiegel, das bedeutet, daß es häufig bergab geht und nur selten bergauf.

The route follows an old smuggling and shepherds track through the Holomondas mountains. The starting point for the walk is the beautiful village square at Taxiarchis. Here stands a marble monument to a war hero:
Ioannis Parliaris
Hero of Macedonia
(1903 -1913).

Die Route geht auf einem alten Schmuggler- und Hirtenpfad durch das Holomondas Gebirge. Ausgangspunkt der Wanderung ist der große Dorfplatz von Taxiarchis. Hier steht eine Marmorstatue von:
Ioannis Parliaris,
einem Mazedonischen Kriegshelden
(1903 - 1913).

From the memorial take the road that leads northeast between the houses, leading to the church. Continue on the road out of town until, after 250m we come to the end of the tarmac road, which bends away to the right. At this point turn left (look for the waymarker), pass to the left of a hut with a corrugated iron roof, then through a hole in the hedge, and down a steep bank of loose packed soil (care

Vom Denkmal aus gehen Sie auf der Straße zwischen den Häusern Richtung Nordosten, zur Kirche. Der Weg führt Sie aus der Stadt hinaus und nach 250m ist die Asphaltstraße zu Ende und führt nach rechts. Sie halten sich links (schauen Sie nach dem Wegweiser), gehen an einer Hütte mit einem Wellblechdach vorbei, durch eine Lücke in der Hecke und einen steilen Abhang mit umgebrochenen, beim

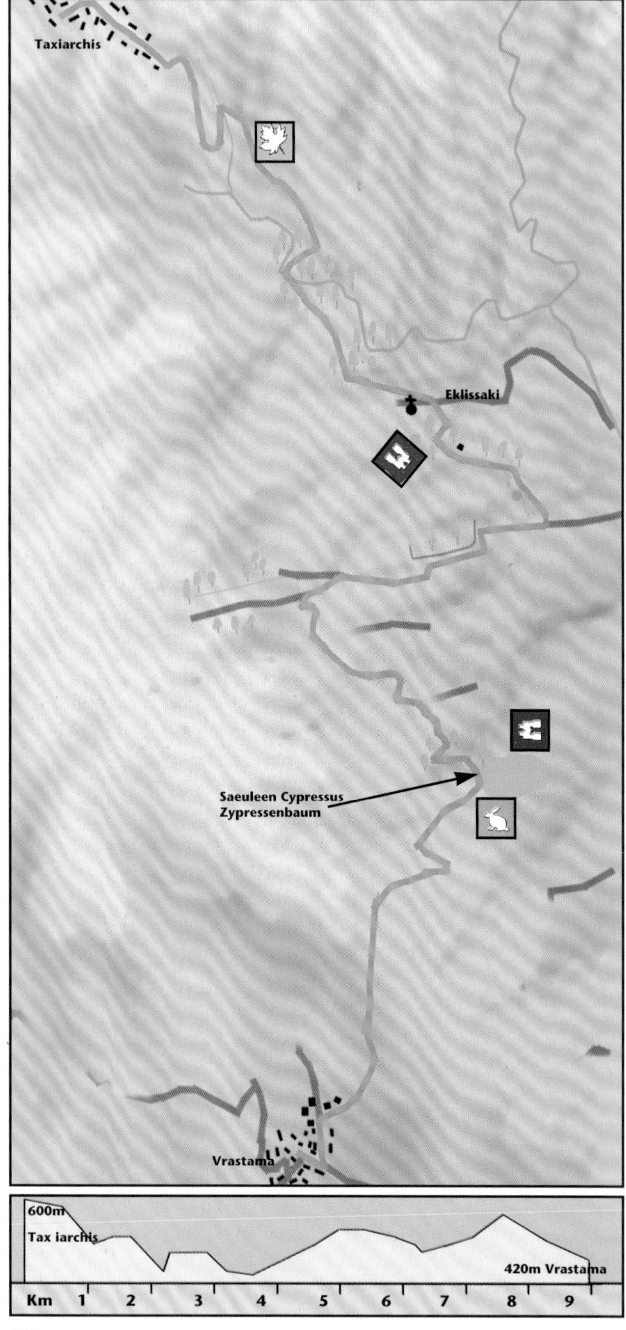
Taxiarchis
Eklissaki
Saeuleen Cypressus
Zypressenbaum
Vrastama
600m
Tax iarchis
420m Vrastama
Km 1 2 3 4 5 6 7 8 9

needed). This leads directly onto a narrow shepherds path leading southwest, which was also a smuggling route in the past. Turn right onto this track, which meanders down the side of the valley through scrub and woodland. On the way edible chestnut trees are seen, together with fine views of the valley ahead and to the left. The gradual descent continues, with occasional reversals of direction as the miniature gorges cut out by streams in wet weather are traversed. Eventually, after a kilometre or so, the bottom of the gorge is reached, a shady stream is crossed, and the path begins to ascend the other side. However in the next 800m only twenty metres of height are gained, as we traverse across the valley. The vegetation becomes more open, allowing fine views of Taxiarchis above and to the right of us. In the next 200m the route swings to the west and descends to a flat area, well shaded by trees, with a clear stream running through it. This is an ideal place to stop for a lunch break or rest awhile.

From here the path crosses the stream and climbs the bank at the other side; heading in a southeasterly direction. After 200m or so the path, which is now passing through dense undergrowth, reaches a clearing and drops down to a dry stream bed. A much larger clearing, on a rise, is reached after another 400m of mainly level walking. Looking back from here Taxiarchis can be seen standing prominently; high on the hill behind us.

The path continues to climb, now in an easterly direction,

Pflügen entstanden Erdschollen hinunter (Vorsicht!). So kommen Sie zu einem engen Hirtenpfad, der früher auch als Schmugglerpfad diente. Biegen Sie rechts auf diesen Pfad Richtung Südwesten ein und wandern Sie die Bergflanke durch Büsche und Bäume abwärts. Unterwegs sehen Sie Ess-Kastanienbäume und genießen Sie die herrliche Aussicht auf das Tal, das sich zu Ihrer linken ausbreitet. Es geht geradlinig bergab, nur ab und zu wechselt der Weg seine Richtung, immer wenn Sie kleine Gruben, die bei Regen durch das strömende Wasser entstanden sind, umgehen müssen. Nach ungefähr 1km erreichen Sie endlich den Grund der Schlucht, überqueren einen im Schatten liegenden Bach und steigen auf der anderen Seite hinauf. Auf den nächsten 800m werden Sie nur 20m an Höhe gewinnen, weil der Pfad durch das Tal führt. Die Landschaft wird offener und Sie können nach Taxiarchis, das sich oben rechts befindet, hinaufblicken. Nach 200m führt die Route nach Westen zu einer kleinen Ebene abwärts. Ein Bach mit klarem Wasser fließt duch die schattenspendenden Bäume; ein idealer Platz für eine Mittagspause oder eine kleine Rast.

Der Pfad überquert den Bach und klettert den Hang auf der anderen Seite, Richtung Südosten, hinauf. Nach ca. 200m durch das dichte Unterholz kommen Sie auf eine Lichtung und steigen dann zu einem ausgetrockneten Flußbett ab. Nach weiteren 400m auf ebener Strecke erreichen Sie eine größere Lichtung, an einem

Colourful Vegetation on the Taxiarchis walk

Farbenprächtige Landschaft in Taxiarchis

to cross a farm road at a high point, where there is an Eklissaki (little church). Turn left onto this track for 30m and look for a way marker on the right to indicate the next section of the route, which meanders down the hill in a generally southerly direction. In 200m or so a well shaded stream bed is reached and the path swings east of south, crosses another stream bed and emerges into an open area, where a ruined building can be seen to the left. Soon after crossing yet another dry streambed the path rises through a large clearing in the bush. Here the way is rather indistinct on the ground, as it continues upwards, due east. Eventually, nearly 400m after the last streambed, a small perfectly circular clearing is reached. This is an old charcoal burners hearth, where charcoal was once made. The path carries straight on in a southwesterly direction as it rises to a minor summit in a further 250m.

Hang. Wenn Sie nach hinten schauen, sehen Sie deutlich Taxiarchis hoch oben auf dem Berg.

Wandern Sie Richtung Osten weiter, bis zu einem Feldweg an einem Eklissaki (kleine Kapelle), wo Sie links abbiegen. Nach 30m sehen Sie rechts ein Wegschild, dem Sie auf der nächsten Etappe der Wanderung, bergab Richtung Süden, folgen. Nach 200m kommen Sie an einen schattigen Fluß, der Weg führt nun nach Osten, und Sie überqueren erneut einen Fluß, bis Sie an einen Punkt kommen, wo sich zu Ihrer linken ein eingefallenes Gebäude befindet. Nachdem Sie noch ein ausgetrocknetes Bachbett überquert haben, erreichen Sie eine Lichtung und anschließend wieder die Büsche auf der anderen Seite. Der nicht deutlich erkennbare Weg führt abwärts, Richtung Osten. Nach 400m vom letzten Flußbett entfernt erreichen Sie eine kreisförmige Lichtung, eine Feuerstelle, auf der früher die

Here there are fine views to the left, with varied and colourful vegetation all around. The route now descends through an oak wood to reach a wide forest road in 250m. Tortoises can be seen wandering here. Turn right onto the road, which rises to the southwest until a wire fence is reached; in 500m or so. The road keeps to the left of the fence, bearing southwest to reach the top of a rise; where it divides into two. Our path follows the left-hand branch, which gradually descends across open land to rise again. About 300m from the fork in the road look to your left for a waymarker. This indicates the start of the next section of the route, a small track leading off into the wood on the left. This path travels eastward and then swings round towards the south to cross a farm track after 200m. It then meanders southeast through shady woods for another 600m, at which point it reaches a wide forest road. After crossing the road the path begins a gradual descent through bushy undergrowth to reach a streambed. It then rises to an open plateau in 600m or so. Here a single tall Saeuleen Cupressus, stands amidst huge piles of cut timber ready for winter (in October). It can be very rewarding to carefully observe the local flora and fauna here. On my last visit a member of the group pointed out a large green praying mantis on a small bush, which I photographed of course. About 100m southeast of the large tree look for a broad and rocky farm track leading off to the right. This climbs to the southwest taking us out of

Holzkohle hergestellt wurde. Der Weg geht geradeaus weiter Richtung Südwesten und kommt nach 250m auf einem Hügel an. Ein schönes, farbenfrohes Bild mit vielfältiger Vegetation breitet sich vor Ihnen aus. Jetzt gehen Sie durch einen Eichenwald und treffen nach 250m eine breite Forststraße. Vielleicht gesellen sich einige Schidkröten zu Ihnen. Biegen Sie rechts ab und gehen Sie Richtung Südwesten, bis Sie nach 500m einen Maschendrahtzaun sehen. Die Straße geht links am Zaun entlang und teilt sich oben auf der Kuppe in zwei Abzweigungen. Gehen Sie auf dem linken Pfad, geradewegs durch offenes Land, bis der Weg wieder ansteigt. Nach 300m sehen Sie einen Wegweiser, der die nächste Etappe der Route ankündigt. Es geht auf einem kleinen Pfad links in den Wald hinein, Richtung Osten. Dann führt unser Weg nach Süden und überquert nach 200m einen Feldweg. Wandern Sie jetzt etwa 600m durch schattigen Wald bis zu einer breiten Forststraße. Überqueren Sie die Straße und gehen Sie geradeaus durch das Gestrüpp, bis zu einem Bach hinunter. Dann erscheint nach 600m ein weites Plateau, auf dem ein hoher Zypressenbaum, mitten zwischen gehacktem Winterholz, steht. Es lohnt sich wirklich, die hiesige Flora und Fauna genau zu betrachten. Bei meinem letzten Besuch entdeckte ein Mitglied der Gruppe eine große, grüne Gottesanbeterin (Fangheuschrecke) auf einem kleinen Busch, die ich natürlich fotografiert habe. 100m vom großen Baum entfernt,

the valley, to cross a road after 1000m or so. The route continues south on a narrow track, which winds through holly bushes and descends to arrive at a clearing in 500m. From the clearing the path meets a ploughed field, which we skirt round on the left side, and make for a red roofed building in front. This building is part of the recently constructed recreation area, which is attached to the local church on the outskirts of Vrastama. The church, which in spite of its external appearance is quite old, is well worth a visit. From here it is an easy stroll down to the centre of the village, where there are two Tavernas.

A Preying Mantis seen on a bush near the Saeuleen Cupressus tree

Eine Gottesanbeterin auf einem Strauch bei dem Zypressenbaum

Richtung Südosten, finden Sie einen breiten, steinigen Feldweg, der nach rechts führt. Sie wandern jetzt südwärts aus dem Tal hinaus und überqueren nach 1km eine weitere Straße. Es geht weiter Richtung Süden auf einem engen Pfad, der nach 500m durch stacheliges Gebüsch auf eine Lichtung führt. Von dort gehen Sie auf dem Pfad weiter, bis Sie zu einem gerodeten Feld kommen. Gehen Sie links um das Feld herum bis zu einem Gebäude mit einem roten Dach. Es gehört zu dem neulich geschaffenen Versammlungsplatz, der zusammen mit der Dorfkirche am Rande von Vrastama liegt. Es lohnt sich, die Kirche, die äußerlich nicht besonders interessant aussieht, aber sehr alt ist, zu besichtigen. Von hieraus finden Sie leicht Ihren Weg hinunter in die Dorfmitte, wo sich zwei Tavernen befinden.

Taxiarchis

Vrastrama - Ag. Efthimios - Vrastama

This walk is quite arduous and difficult in places requiring good footwear, and should not be attempted after heavy rainfall. The walk starts in the high mountain village of Vrastama and follows an unsurfaced road over the hill behind the village to descend along a narrow ridge into the large valley beyond. The many deep ravines cutting through the valley restrict the possibilities for easy progress and it is necessary in places to descend into the beds of streams and follow water courses.

Diese Wanderung ist anstrengend und schwierig, und sollte nicht nach starken Regenfällen unternommen werden. Gutes Schuhwerk ist erforderlich.
Ausgangspunkt ist das hochgelegene Bergdorf Vrastama. Von dort folgen Sie einer unbefestigten Straße über den Berg hinter dem Dorf und steigen einen langen, schmalen Kamm abwärts in das weite Tal. Viele, tiefe Schluchten versperren Ihnen den Weg und machen es Ihnen nicht leicht, voran zu kommen. Zum Teil müssen Sie an einigen Stellen in das Flußbett absteigen und dem Wasserlauf folgen.

The highlight of the walk is a visit to a natural cave, *Ag. Efithimios* at the bottom of a remote ravine. This was once the home of a hermit, and is now a shrine.

Der Höhepunkt dieser Wanderung ist die Besichtigung der abgelegenen Höhle *Agios Efthimios,* die auf dem Grund einer abgelegenen Schlucht liegt. Hier lebte einst ein Einsiedler, heute ist es eine heilige Stätte.

There are two possibilities for this walk. The first is a one way journey from Vrastama to Ag. Efthimios and then on to the road near the village of Plana. This has the advantage that one does not have to re-ascend out of the ravine,

Es gibt zwei Alternativen für diese Wanderung. Die erste Möglichkeit ist, von Vrastama zu Agios Efthimios und dann zur Straße nahe bei Plana zu wandern. Das hat den Vorteil, daß Sie nicht wieder aus der Schlucht hinaufklettern müssen, aber dafür müssen Sie für den Rücktransport nach Vra-

but the disadvantage that transport will need to be arranged for the return to Vrastama.

stama vorsorgen.

The second possibility is to visit Ag. Efthimios and then return to Vrastrama by following a different route back; which makes use of goat trails to climb through the bush.

Die zweite Möglichkeit ist, Ag. Efthimios zu besichtigen und nach Vrastama zurückzuwandern.

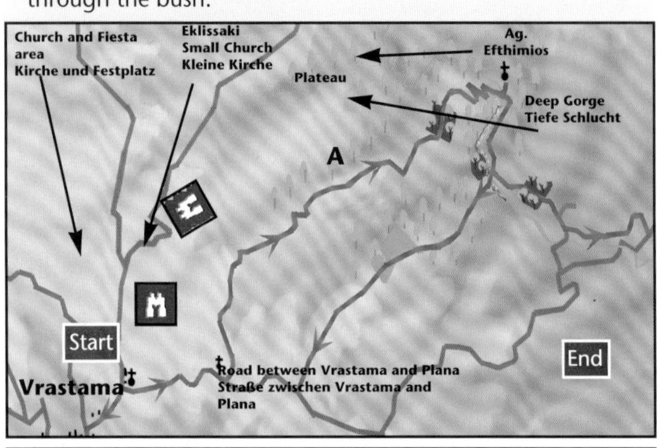

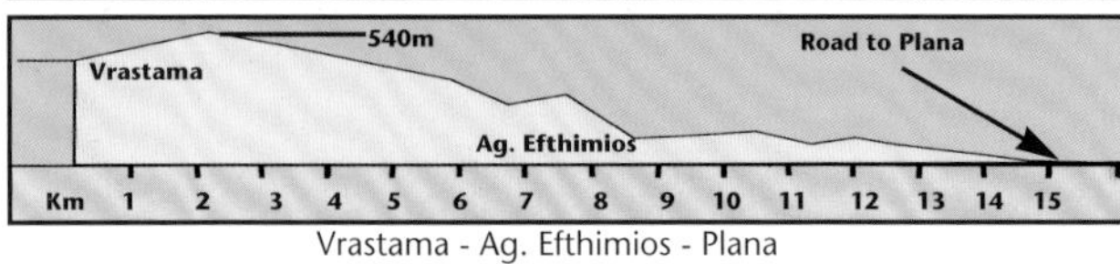

Vrastama - Ag. Efthimios - Plana

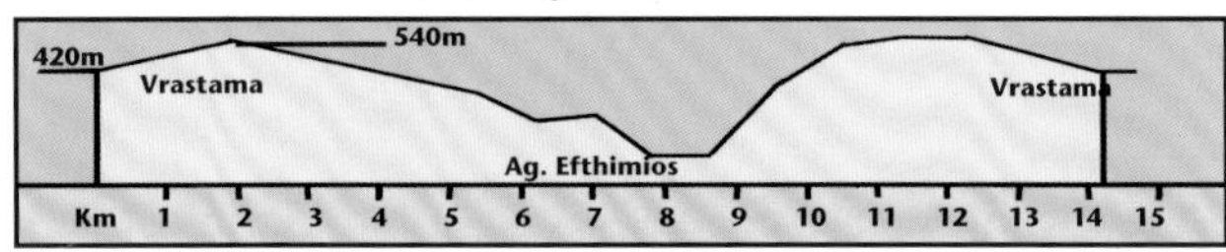

Vrastama - Ag. Efthimios - Vrastama

The start of the walk is the road junction opposite the school in Vrastama. Follow the road which rises to the west directly opposite the school. In a couple of hundred metres a junction is reached with a water trough on ground to the left. Take the right fork, which leads past a large red Eklissaki up to the beautiful little church,

Ausgangspunkt der Wanderung ist die Kreuzung gegenüber der Schule in Vrastama. Folgen Sie der Straße, die gegenüber der Schule Richtung Westen ihren Anfang hat. Nach ein paar hundert Metern kommen Sie an eine Gabelung, wo links ein Wassertrog steht. Nehmen Sie die Abzweigung rechts und gehen Sie, vorbei

with its fountain and picnic tables. To continue follow the road leading east and up the hill, with the church on your left. This track quickly gains height and provides beautiful panoramic views of the countryside to the right. After half a kilometre or so the track bears right, past another Ekliassis to reach a junction. Turn left here onto a new track (signposted *Ag. Efthimios)* which breasts the ridge to descend into the large valley down one of the many small ridges that radiate down the valley's length. Magnificent views are to be had from here of the whole valley ahead and to the left. The town nestling high on the hillside to the north is Taxiarchis. Directly ahead, in the distance, can be seen a plateau of land linked to the end of the ridge that we are descending. After one kilometre of easy walking the path bears right and then left to approach this table top of land. The route passes through an olive grove, then climbs to the highest point, where it comes to a sudden end, with steep wooded cliffs on three sides. The way forward is indicated by another signpost to *Ag. Efthimio*s which points to a small track descending the steep cliff face to the east. This narrow, but good, track zig zags down into the ravine. As the bottom is approached a large white wooden cross can be seen high on the opposite cliff ahead. This marks the position of the shrine which we are approaching. Soon the path arrives in an open space at the bottom of the ravine. Makeshift tables and benches are provided, in this lonely spot for feast days, making it

an einem großen roten Eklissaki, hinauf zu der schönen kleinen Kirche mit ihrem Springbrunnen und Picknicktischen. Links an der Kirche geht der Weg weiter Richtung Osten den Berg hinauf. Sie gewinnen schnell an Höhe und haben einen großartigen Panoramablick auf die Landschaft zu Ihrer rechten. Nach ca. 500m kommen Sie an einem anderen Eklissaki vorbei zu einer Kreuzung. Biegen Sie links ab, auf einen neuen Pfad (beschildert), der den Bergrücken abwärts in das weite Tal führt. Viele kleine Rücken gehen sternförmig vom Tal aus. Der Ort, der harmonisch in die Landschaft eingebettet ist, ist Taxiarchis. Wenn Sie geradeaus in die Ferne schauen, sehen Sie einen Rücken, der sich dem Gebirgsrücken, den Sie hinuntersteigen, anschließt. Nach 1km leichter Wanderung wendet sich der Weg nach rechts und dann nach links, bis Sie ein Plateau erreichen. Der Weg geht durch einen Olivenhain, führt aufwärts auf den höchsten Punkt und endet ganz plötzlich an einem dicht bewachsenen Hang der auf allen drei Seiten steil abfällt. Ein Wegweiser zeigt den Weg nach Agios Efthimios an. Sie steigen auf einem kleinen Weg Richtung Osten den steilen Hang hinab. Es ist ein schmaler, aber guterhaltener Weg, der zickzackförmig die Schlucht hinunterführt. Wenn Sie den Grund der Schlucht erreichen, sehen Sie ein großes, weißes Kreuz gegenüber auf einem Felsen. Direkt darüber befindet sich die Walfahrtststätte Agios Efthimios. Sobald Sie dort angekommen sind, sehen Sie

a good spot for lunch. To visit the grotto of Ag. Efthimios cross the bridge and walk along the left side of the stream for about 60m, where a narrow path will be seen climbing up to the left. This leads directly to the cave, which is accessed by wooden steps. Return to the stream by the same route. From here there are two options.

1.- to carry on to reach the road leading to Plana
(Only do this if you have arranged transport at the other end)
2. - to return to Vrastama

1. To continue to Plana, follow the left hand bank of the stream in the direction it is flowing. At the bend cross the stream and follow the path on the right hand side, which may involve scrambling over some of the large rocks in the stream. After 200m or so the stream bends sharp left, where there is a wall ahead, directly under the rock face (Point **A** on the map above). Depending on the depth of water, either walk along the wall or along the stream bed. Follow the left bank of the stream for a distance of about 100m, whilst looking for a narrow track which rises to the left. Look for the waymarker sign on a tree. Ascend this path which rises up from the stream but continues to follow it for a while. Keep left at the junction which is reached in about 100m. The path now enters an olive grove and crosses the southern edge to arrive at a large tree in the top right hand corner. The path has now become a farm track and meanders up and down in a

View of the plateau above Ag. Efthimios. The arrow indicates the start of the descent into the gorge.

Blick von dem Plateau über Ag. Efthimios. Der Pfeil zeigt den Anfang des Abstiegs in die Schlucht.

provisorische Tische und Bänke, die nur an Festtagen benutzt werden. Hier können Sie eine Mittagspause machen. Um die Höhle von Agios Efthimios zu besichtigen, gehen Sie über die Brücke und links am Fluß ca. 60m entlang, bis zu einem engen Pfad, der links hinaufführt und dann auf Holzstufen direkt in die Höhle leitet. Kehren Sie auf dem gleichen Weg zum Fluß zurück. Ab hier gibt es zwei Möglichkeiten:

1. zur Straße, die nach Plana führt, zu wandern (nur wenn Sie für ein Transportmittel vorgesorgt haben)
2. nach Vrastama zurückzukehren

1. Um nach Plana zu kommen, gehen Sie am linken Ufer des Flußes entlang, immer dem Flußlauf folgend. Überqueren Sie den Fluß in der Windung, indem Sie dem rechten Pfad folgen, wobei Sie über einige große Steine im Fluß steigen müssen. Nach 200m ändert der Fluß plötzlich seine

Ag. Efthimios

south easterly direction for a further 500m, when a track joins from the left on a curve. Keep on the main track, which continues its gradual descent down the side of the valley for a further 300m. to arrive at a junction. Here turn sharp left onto the smaller track, which leads to an orchard in about 70m. Turn sharp right here to find a small track which descends a slope then winds its way along below the orchard, where the flora and fauna are much more interesting. After 200m this path reaches an open cultivated area. Pass round the bottom edge of the garden and follow the right side up to a field, across which is a freshwater spring, with a cup hanging from a pole. One hundred metres further on the path becomes a broad sandy track, which is followed to a junction with a thorn bush at its centre. Keep

Richtung nach links, auf eine Wand im Vordergrund zu, direkt unter einer Felsnase. (Punkt **A** auf der Landkarte).Je nach Wassertiefe gehen Sie entweder an der Wand oder am Flußbett entlang. Gehen Sie 100m am linken Ufer des Flußes entlang, während Sie nach einer engen Fährte auf der linken Seite suchen. Schauen Sie nach dem Wegweiser an einem Baum. Folgen Sie dem Weg, der nach oben führt, aber noch einige Meter parallel zum Fluß verläuft. Nach 100m erreichen Sie eine Abzweigung. Gehen Sie links weiter in einen Olivenhain, den Sie an seiner südlichen Seite überqueren, bis Sie zu einem großen Baum am rechten, oberen Ende des Hains kommen. Der Weg weitet sich zu einer Straße und führt auf und ab, über 500m in südöstliche Richtung, bis von der rechten

left here and then, in 50m, keep right at the next junction. The track now meanders up and down gradually gaining height for a further 350m to arrive at another junction.
Here take the lower path, which descends to the right, bringing you in a further half kilometre to an olive grove. Carry on, due east, straight across the top end of the grove, and through the middle of the next grove. The track continues on to arrive at a church with roofed picnic tables and fiesta area. This is a fine place to stop for refreshment and the church is well worth visiting. The path now descends to the west of the church and then swings sharply round to the south, passing beneath it. Three hundred metres further on young olive trees are passed as the path bears right towards a small building. Turn right at the tree and then left at the next building, which has a stream flowing through a tunnel in its wall. Ahead there is a large stone to the left and a large tree in front. The path turns left at the tree and follows the stream. To the right is the stream with a high earth bank on the opposite side. A little further on the track fords the stream. To keep your feet dry in wet weather, cross by the large stones to the left of the ford. The track now rises to the right away from the stream only to meet it again 200m further on, with an impressive clay cliff face on the opposite side. Here bear right and cross the ford, then follow the track for a further 300m, at which point the stream passes through a tunnel in a very large embankment. The track

Seite ein Pfad auf die Straße einmündet. Bleiben Sie auf der Straße, die weiter geradeaus das Tal hinunterführt. Nach 300m kommen Sie an eine Kreuzung. Hier biegen Sie scharf nach links auf einen kleineren Weg, der zu einem Obstgarten führt, wo die Flora und Fauna sehr interessant ist. Nach 200m kommen Sie auf ein weites Feld. Gehen Sie am unteren Rand der Felder entlang und biegen Sie nach rechts ab. Gegenüber ist ein Trinkwasserbrunnen mit einer Wasserkelle, die an einem Pfahl hängt, zu sehen. Nach 100m wird der Weg breit und sandig und kommt zu einer Gabelung, auf der ein Dornbusch steht. Biegen Sie nach links ab und nach 50m an der nächsten Gabelung rechts. Die nächsten 350m verläuft der Weg auf und ab bis zu einer anderen Kreuzung. Gehen Sie auf dem untenliegenden Weg, der nach rechts auf einen Olivenhain in 1km Entfernung hinunterführt. Gehen Sie ostwärts zum Ende des Hains und dann mitten durch den nächsten, bis zu einer Kirche mit überdachten Picknicktischen und einer Tanzfläche. Machen Sie eine kleine Erfrischungspause und besichtigen Sie die Kirche. Es lohnt sich! Der Weg führt westlich der Kirche abwärts und biegt dann scharf nach Süden, unterhalb der Kirche vorbei. 300m weiter kommen Sie an jungen Olivenbäumen vorbei, rechtshaltend auf ein kleines Gebäude zu. Biegen Sie rechts am Baum ab, und am nächsten Gebäude wieder links, wo ein Fluß durch einen Tunnel in der Wand fließt. Vor Ihnen steht ein großer Baum und links ein großer Stein.

climbs to the left up this embankment. Descend the other side and follow the track past a pig farm and on down the valley for a further 2km. In the last 300m it is necessary to ford the stream again to eventually emerge on the unsurfaced road leading to Plana. Here your transport back to Vrastama should be waiting, if you have pre-booked it.

2. To return to Vrastama from Ag. Efthimios
Take the route downstream to wards Plana as far as point **A** on the map, where the path to Plana climbs away from the streambed. Directly opposite this point is a similar path climbing up the righthand bank, past large trees and through a gap between two sections of rockface. This is an ancient muletrack and in places parts of the original stone road can be seen. Follow this route as it climbs, through dense bush, due

Crossing the stream by the large stones to the left of the ford

Seichte Übergangsstelle über den Fluß, links von den großen Steinen

Der Weg biegt links vom Baum ab und folgt dem Fluß. Rechts befindet sich der Fluß mit seinem steilen Ufer auf der gegenüberliegenden Seite. Etwas weiter auf dem Weg müssen Sie den Fluß durchwatten. Damit Sie nicht naß werden, überqueren Sie den Fluß auf den großen Steinen. Der Weg führt Sie rechts vom Fluß weg und nach 200m wieder in seine Nähe, wo Sie gegenüber seine eindrucksvolle, Lehmwand sehen können. Biegen Sie nach rechts und gehen Sie durch den Fluß, folgen Sie dem Weg 300m, bis zu einem Tunnel, der unter einem großen Straßendamm hindurchführt. Gehen Sie links den Damm hinauf und auf der anderen Seite wieder hinunter, und gehen Sie auf dem Weg 2km, vorbei an einer Schweinzucht, weiter das Tal hinaus. Auf den letzten 300m müssen Sie erneut den Fluß überqueren, bevor Sie auf die Straße, die nach Plana führt, kommen. Hier müßte ihr vorbestelltes Transportmittel auf Sie warten.

2. Um von Agios Efthimios nach Vrastama zurückzukehren, folgen Sie der Route flußabwärts Richtung Plana, bis zu Punkt **A** auf der Landkarte, wo der Weg nach Plana vom Fluß wegführt. Direkt gegenüber führt ein ähnlicher Weg die rechte Uferbank hinauf, vorbei an großen Bäumen und durch einen Spalt zwischen zwei Bruchstücken eines senkrechten Felsens. Das ist ein alter Maultierweg, und stellenweise kann man auch Teile der ursprünglichen Pflasterung sehen. Folgen Sie dieser Route, die Sie durch

south out of the gorge. In about 400m the path swings towards the west and emerges into open ground. The route now leads west to re-enter the bush in about 40m (look for the waymarker). In a further 360m a large tree is reached with a small stream just beyond it. There should be a Poseidon symbol nailed to the tree. This indicates the start of a narrow goat track, climbing up through the bush, immediately behind the tree. Follow this track which meanders up through dense bushland for about 300m to emerge into the corner of a large open field.
Follow the hedge on the left, the south side, in order to ascend the hill to the top of the field. Here there is a smaller field with a broad mountain track beyond, which ascends to the top of the ridge. Cross the field onto the track but, before continuing, look back for a panoramic view over the whole valley.
Now continue up the track for a distance of 1200m to attain the ridge. From here turn right and follow the track back down towards Vrastama. After 300m or so the junction is reached with an *Eklissaki*, where you turned off for Ag. Efthimios, earlier in the day. Continue on, down the main track back to Vrastama.

dichte Büsche aus der Schlucht Richtung Süden hinaufführt. Nach 400m wendet sich der Pfad nach Westen und mündet in eine Lichtung ein. Jetzt geht es wieder westwärts und nach 40m zurück in die Büsche (achten Sie auf den Wegweiser). Nach ca. 350m erreichen Sie einen großen Baum, hinter dem ein Bach fließt. Ein Poseidon Wegweiser müßte an dem Baum festgenagelt sein. Hier unmittelbar hinter dem Baum beginnt eine schmaler Ziegenpfad, der die Böschung hinaufführt. Folgen Sie diesem Pfad durch das dichte Gebüsch, bis Sie nach 300m auf einem offenen Feld angelangen.
Gehen Sie an der Hecke, die südliche Seite des Feldes entlang, und steigen Sie auf den Hügel, dem oberen Ende des Feldes. Hier befindet sich ein kleineres Feld, von dem ein breiter Weg auf einen Höhenrücken führt. Gehen Sie über das Feld auf diese Straße, und bevor Sie weiterlaufen, werfen Sie einen Blick zurück auf das ganze Tal.
Wandern Sie jetzt eine Entfernung von ca. 1,2km aufwärts, um den Berg zu ersteigen. Oben angelangt biegen Sie nach rechts und folgen dem Weg, der zurück nach Vrastama führt. Nach 300m erreichen Sie eine Gabelung mit einem *Eklissaki* in der Ecke. Hier sind Sie auf dem Hinweg nach Agios Efthimios abgebogen. Auf der Hauptstraße gehen Sie abwärts, zurück nach Vrastama.

Holomondas - Paleochora

This long walk starts almost at the summit of Mt. Holomondas above the village of Taxiarchis and then descends through remote terrain to the village of Paleochora, 10km to the northwest. The route follows modern forest tracks as well as much older mule tracks in its gradual descent through beautiful forest, bush and farmland.

Diese lange Wanderung beginnt fast auf dem höchsten Punkt des Holomondas - Gebirges, oberhalb des Dorfes Taxiarchis und führt dann durch abgelegene Gebiete in das Dorf Paleochora, 10km nordwestlich, hinunter. Die Route nutzt sowohl Forststraßen, als auch alte Maultierpfade, und verläuft durch wunderschöne Mischwälder, Buschland und über fruchtbare Äcker.

The start of the route is a forest track on the left hand side of the road from Taxiarchis to Arnea, approximately 3.3 km north of the junction of the road to Arnea with the road leading down into the village of Taxiarchis. Look for the waymarker sign which should be prominently displayed.

Ausgangspunkt der Wanderung ist ein Waldweg, der auf der linken Seite der Straße von Taxiarchis nach Arnea, ungefähr 3km nördlich der kleinen Kirche Profitis Ilias, ausgeht. Achten Sie auf die Wegweiser.

Follow the forest track that descends to the northwest as it clings to the western slopes of Holomondas. If the weather is clear there is a fine view to the left, over the forest and across to Mount Olympus in the far background. In 600m, at a fork in the track, take the upper path (waymarker). One hundred metres further on an open area is reached with fine views to the southwest. Here the path turns sharply to the north, passing to the right of a concrete water reservoir and

Folgen Sie dem Waldweg Richtung Nordwesten und steigen Sie den Westhang des Holomondas ab. Wenn das Wetter klar ist, haben Sie eine herrliche Aussicht auf den Wald zu Ihrer linken und den Olymp im Hintergrund. Nach 600m kommen Sie an eine Abzweigung. Nehmen Sie den oberen Pfad (siehe Wegweiser). 100m weiter erreichen Sie eine Lichtung, die schöne Ausblicke nach Südwesten gewährt. Hier dreht der Pfad scharf nach

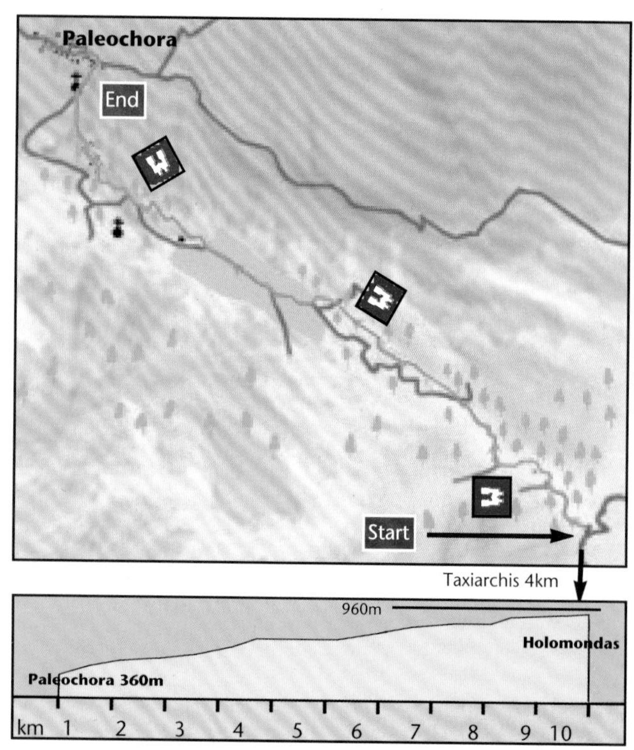

entering thicker woodland. Follow the waymarkers for the next 400m, as the path contours round the hillside through fairly dense woodland. As an open area is reached the route leaves the path we are on and turns to the north (follow the waymarkers). In another 500m or so the route emerges from the woodland onto a wide forest track, which is joined for a few metres to a corner. The route now leaves the track, dropping down the hillside to the west and passing a fenced compound in which Christmas trees are grown. Most of the Christmas trees sold in Greece come from this area. Soon the road is reached again, but we

Norden, kommt an einem Wasserreservoir aus Beton vorbei und führt Sie in den dichten Wald hinein. Folgen Sie auf den nächsten 400m immer den Wegweisern, denn der Weg führt durch dichten Wald. An einer lichten Stelle im Wald verlassen Sie den Weg, auf dem Sie sich gerade befinden, und folgen einem weiteren nach Norden (folgen Sie den Wegweisern). Nach weiteren 500m mündet der Weg in eine breite Forststraße ein, auf der Sie einige Meter bis zu einer Kurve gehen. Dort verlassen Sie die Straße wieder und steigen den Berg Richtung Westen hinunter, bis zu einem Gehege, wo Tannen-bäume angepflanzt werden. Die meisten Weihnachts-

continue on a quiet forest track to the right, ignoring a left fork into a field. In 150m or so locked gates block the track (another Christmas tree nursery). Turn left here and follow the fence round, through the trees for a further 300 m or so. Continue on a further 50m, along the left hand edge of a ploughed field, to arrive at an open top, giving fine views to the north. The route now follows a small, but beautiful, shrub and gorse covered ridge,

(**Photo above**),which descends gradually to the northwest. In 500m the ridge levels out, crosses a farm track and continues on through the bushes for a further 100m, when a field begins on the left. Cross over at the top end of the field (to avoid damage to crops) onto the main farm road. The route follows this road for the next 900m, through the cornfields. At the end of the fields a little used track drops away to the right, away from the road (look for the waymarker). This is an old mule track to Paleochora, which we will join and leave several times during the remainder of the journey. The route continues westward for 500m before turning to

bäume kommen aus dieser Gegend. Bald kommen Sie wieder auf die Straße, bis unser Weg nach rechts weiterführt. Lassen Sie den Weg, der nach links in ein Feld hinter sich. Nach 150m ist die Straße durch ein Tor versperrt (ein weitere Tannenbaum-Anpflanzung). Biegen Sie hier links und gehen Sie um den Zaun herum, etwa 300m durch Bäume. Gehen Sie weitere 50m am linken Rand eines gerodeten Feldes entlang, bis Sie auf einem Hügel mit hervorragender Aussicht nach Norden anlangen. Die Route führt jetzt durch eine mit Büschen und Stechginstersträuchern bedeckte Schlucht, die nach Nordwesten verläuft. (Photo links). Nach 500m läuft die Schlucht aus. Sie überqueren einen Feldweg und gehen weiter durch die Büsche, bis Sie nach 100m auf ein Feld kommen. Überqueren Sie das Feld am oberen Rande (um nicht auf die Saat zu treten), bis zum Hauptweg. Sie gehen jetzt die nächsten 900m auf dieser Straße zwischen den Feldern hindurch. Am Ende der Felder angelangt zweigen Sie von der Straße nach rechts ab und folgen dem kleinen, ausgewaschenen Weg nach unten. (siehe Wegweiser). Das ist ein alter Maultierpfad, auf dem der größte Teil der restlichen Strecke verläuft. Die Route führt westwärts weiter, dreht nach 500m nach Süden und verbindet sich mit einem Feldweg. Gehen Sie links auf diesem Feldweg etwa 200m um ein kleines Tal herum und etwas aufwärts. Hier erscheint wieder der alte Eselspfad und Sie gehen weitere 400m auf ihm, bis zu einem Ziegenpferch. Die alte Route führt

Holomondas - Paleochora in January *(im Januar)*

the south and rejoining a farm road. Follow this farm road to the left for 200m, around the head of the valley and up the hill. Here the old track re-appears on the right and we follow it for 400m to arrive at a goat shelter. The old route continues on down through a rocky gully. The original path has been mostly washed away over the years during wet weather, but in several places the old stone set surface of the road can be seen. After 800m of descent this ancient road meets up with a modern track, which we join. 200m further on is a water reservoir and in a further 100m we arrive at another church, dedicated to the Prophet Elias, situated just above the village of Paleochora. Follow the road to the right of the church, which leads down into the village, where there are several taverna's. Here you can explore or rest a while, before booking a taxi back to Holomondas.

weiter hinunter durch eine Schlucht. Der ursprüngliche Pfad ist in den letzten Jahren durch die Regenfälle ausgespült worden, aber an manchen Stellen kann man die alte Pflasterung noch sehen. Nach 800m trifft dieser historische Weg auf einen neuen Feldweg, dem Sie folgen. Nach 200m sehen Sie ein Wasserreservoir und nach weiteren 100m kommen Sie an eine Kirche, die dem Propheten Ilias gewidmet ist und direkt oberhalb des Dorfes Paleochora liegt. Folgen Sie der Straße rechts von der Kirche, die hinunter ins Dorf führt, wo es einige Tavernen gibt. Sie können eine Weile rasten oder durch das Dorf bummeln, bevor Sie ein Taxi zurück zum Aussichtspunkt bestellen.

Olympiada - Stagira - Olympiada

This short but interesting walk takes one through the archeological remains of the Ancient City of Stagira, which was situated on the two small hills, overlooking the sea, at the north western corner of Olympiada. It then ascends the hill to the south of the town on a forest track providing a fine woodland walk, with the added bonus of panoramic views over Olympiada and its bay below. A quick descent to the village then follows on a narrow, hunters' path, and the walk ends with a stroll along the beach.

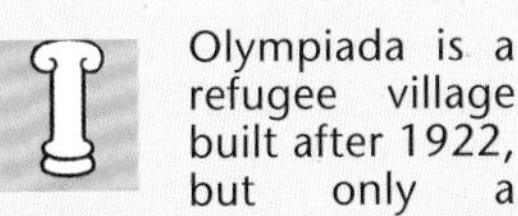

Olympiada is a refugee village built after 1922, but only a kilometre east of the village is the site of the ancient city of Stagira; probably the most important historical site in Halkidiki. During the 7th century B.C. Stagira was colonized first by Andrians and then, later, by Chalceans. The city was taken over by the Persians in the Persian Wars and became a member of the Athenium Alliance. Later in 424 B.C. the city rebelled and joined the Lacedaemonians, causing it to

Diese kurze, aber interessante Wanderung führt Sie zu den archäologischen Funden der antiken Stadt Stagira, die zwischen zwei Hügeln lag. Auf der nordwestlichen Seite von Olympiada haben Sie einen Panoramablick über das Meer. Auf einem Waldpfad steigen Sie anschließend auf den Berg südlich des Orts und wandern durch lichten Wald.

Unterwegs bieten sich herrliche Ausblicke auf das Dorf Olympiada und seine Bucht. Zum Schluß steigen Sie nach Olympiada ab beenden die Wanderung mit einem Spaziergang am Strand.

Olympiada wurde im Jahr 1922 von Flüchtlingen gegründet. Nur 1km östlich befinden sich die Ausgrabungen der antiken Stadt Stagira, vermutlich die wichtigste historische Sehenswürdigkeit auf Chalkidiki. Während des 7. Jahrhunderts v.Chr. siedelten sich hier Bewohner der Insel Andros und der Stadt Halkida an. Die Stadt wurde während der Persischen Kriege von den Persern erobert und trat dem Athener Bund bei. Nach einem Aufstand im Jahre 424 v.Chr. verbündete

be beseiged by the Athenians without success. Stagira later became a member of the Chalcidean League, until it was destroyed in 348 B.C. by Philip; who later rebuilt it in order to honour Artistotle.

sie sich mit den Lakedämoniern und wurde von den Athenern - jedoch ohne Erfolg - besetzt. Stagira war später Mitglied im Chalkidiker Bund. 348 v. Chr. wurde die Stadt von König Philipp zerstört. Er baute sie später zu Ehren von Aristoteles wieder auf.

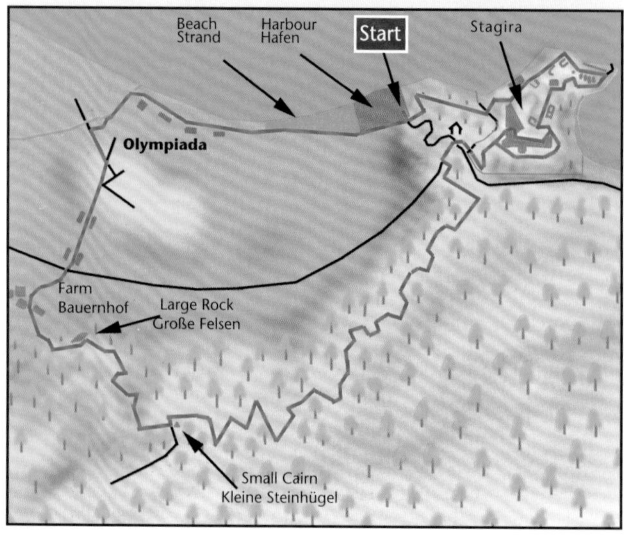

The start point of the walk is the small harbour at the north western corner of the village, where there is adequate parking at most times. From the harbour follow the small track which bears sharp left towards the sea (Look for the Poseidon waymarker). In 60m the track swings west to follow the coast under the cliff on your right to reach locked iron gates in a further distance of 250m or so. The gates are there just to prevent access to vehicles, the pedestrian gate to the right should open. Immediately above and to the right a restored wall descends the

Ausgangspunkt ist der kleine Hafen im Nordwesten des Dorfes, wo es meistens genügend Parkmöglichkeiten gibt. Gehen Sie vom Hafen aus den kleinen Pfad entlang, der scharf links zum Meer führt (schauen Sie nach den Poseidon Wegmarkierungen). Nach 60m biegt der Pfad nach Westen. Gehen Sie 250m rechts unter den Klippen die Küste entlang bis zum verschlossenen Tor. Es verhindert den Zugang für Fahrzeuge, aber die Tür für Fussgänger daneben lässt sich bestimmt öffnen. Direkt darüber auf der rechten Seite verläuft eine restaurierte

hill. The path continues east, with the sea to the left, to arrive at the restored ruins of a building with steps up to a stone floor. This was a church in ancient times.
Footpaths lead up the hill on both sides of the church to reach a curved stone wall, the foundations of various buildings and an ancient reservoir. Continuing on down the other side there is a shrine to Aphrodite, complete with a well. From here follow the stone wall down towards the sea, noting the remains of various buildings on either side. In a short distance another path joins the route. Turn right onto this path and continue round the small peninsula, with the sea to the left below rocks, to arrive at an ancient wall. The path turns parallel to the wall and climbs gently upwards, revealing more ruins to the right in the bushes. At the next path junction, take the lower route to emerge at some steps in 30m or so. Descend the steps and turn right to walk up the section of ancient road. Note the walls of the buildings on the right, including the large earthenware bowl, which was used in winemaking. From here, back at the church, turn left, go up the steps and follow the track south for 150m. On the left between the sea and the track are more remains of the old city, and at the bend in the road, there are steps to access remains above the track. A little further on steps lead up to the old wall that climbs the hill. One can take this route or follow the wide track round the front of the wall. At the top of the hill is a round tower at the southern end of

Mauer den Hügel hinauf. Gehen Sie östlich auf dem Pfad weiter,zu Ihrer linken ist das Meer. Sie kommen jetzt zu einer Ruine, deren Treppe zu einem Steinboden führt. Dies war früher eine Kirche.
Auf beiden Seiten der Kirche führen Trampelpfade den Hügel hinauf bis zu einer schiefen Mauer, Fundamenten von verschiedenen Gebäuden und einem Wasserreservoir. Auf der anderen Seite geht es wieder abwärts zu einem Altar der Göttin Aphrodite. Daneben steht ein Brunnen. Folgen Sie der Steinmauer hinunter zum Meer. Auf beiden Seiten stehen alte Gebäudeteile. Nach kurzer Zeit treffen Sie einen anderen Pfad. Folgen Sie ihm nach rechts, gehen Sie um die kleine Halbinsel herum, während das Meer sich die ganze Zeit links hinter den Felsen befindet. Sie kommen an einer alten Mauer an, wo der Pfad Sie, parallel zu der Mauer, hinaufführt. Weitere Ruinen sind auf der rechten Seite hinter den Büschen zu sehen. An der nächsten Gabelung nehmen Sie den unteren Weg, der nach 30m zu einer Treppe führt. Steigen Sie ab und biegen Sie rechts auf die alte Straße. Beachten Sie die Wände der Gebäude zu Ihrer rechten mit den großen Tonkrügen, die bei der Herstellung von Wein benutzt wurden. Von hier gehen Sie zurück zu der Kirche und folgen dem Pfad 150m südwärts. Zwischen dem Meer und dem Pfad befinden sich auf der linken Seite noch mehr archäologische Funde der alten Stadt. Aus der Kurve leiten Stufen zu den Funden über dem Pfad. Etwas weiter weg führen andere Stufen Sie

the wall and a large triangular open space, with well and other remains. This was the Acropolis of the ancient City of Stagira. There is more to see here and one may wish to spend further time exploring before continuing with the walk.
The walk now continues from the round tower at the top of the hill. Follow the track that leads southwest down the hill towards the main road. There are wooden benches here to rest and observe the view if you wish. In 200m the path emerges through more iron gates onto the main road between Olympiada and Stratoni at a viewpoint above the village. Turn sharp left here onto the road, which bypasses the village centre, and in 50m turn left off this road onto a forest track (waymarker). This track meanders up, through mixed forest, following the twists and turns of the hillside, to the south of Olympiada. There are several points along the route where excellent views are obtained across the valley below. In 300m there is a large concrete water reservoir, which is a good viewpoint, but probably the best view is obtained, after a further 500m of ascent. From this point, where there is almost a 180 degree curve in the track, a panoramic view of the whole valley is seen. Continue on from here, still climbing, for a further 500m or so, until the track levels out on a left hand bend, with a long flat straight in front. Only 15m from this corner a shepherds path descends steeply to the right. A small cairn of stones may mark the way (look for the waymarker). Follow this path down the hill

zu der alten Stadtmauer, die den Hügel emporführt. Entweder steigen Sie diesen Pfad hoch, oder Sie gehen auf dem breiteren Weg an der Vorderseite der Mauer entlang. Oben auf dem Hügel befindet sich am Südende der Mauer ein runder Turm und eine große dreieckige Fläche, mit einem Brunnen und anderen Funden. Hier befand sich die Akropolis der alten Stadt Stagira. Es gibt noch vieles mehr zu sehen und Sie können sich ruhig etwas Zeit für eine Besichtigung nehmen, bevor Sie die Wanderung fortsetzen.
Vom Turm aus folgen Sie jetzt dem Pfad Richtung Südwesten, der zur Hauptstraße führt. Auf den Holzbänken können Sie sich ausruhen und die Aussicht genießen. Nach 200m gehen Sie durch weitere Eisentore. Sie befinden sich jetzt auf dem Weg zur Hauptstraße zwischen Olympiada und Stratoni. Biegen Sie scharf links auf die Hauptrstraße, die das Dorf durchquert, und nach 50m biegen Sie wieder links ab, von der Asphaltstraße auf einen Waldweg (s.Wegschild). Sie wandern jetzt aufwärts durch den Mischwald. Der Weg zur Südseite von Olympiada hat viele Kurven und Biegungen und während Sie den Hang hinaufsteigen, gewährt er Ihnen von manchen Stellen aus herrliche Blicke über das Tal. Nach 300m finden Sie einen großen Wasserspeicher, von dem man eine schöne Aussicht hat. Aber 500m weiter, in einer 180 Grad Kurve, haben Sie einen Panoramablick auf das ganze Tal. Der Weg steigt weiter an, bis er nach ca. 500m in einer Linkskurve eben und gerade

as it twists and turns through the bushes. Look for red and white waymarker bands on the bushes or Poseidon symbols on trees and stones where the route is not obvious. The direction changes from north to west frequently as the path descends. Eventually it passes through more open ground, with large rocks on the right. Soon after, the route enters a farmyard. Pass between the two buildings onto a track which leads round to the right to reach the main road in 200m. Cross straight over onto the sandy track leading into the village of Olympiada. In a further 200m the road rises to a junction. Keep left here to reach a ford crossing a concrete stream bed 100m further on. The path now turns right and follows the stream bed to reach an asphalted road at a bridge. Carry straight on across the road towards the beach, which is directly ahead. On reaching the beach, turn right at the Taverna and continue past the sea front shops and along the beach to the car park.

Olympiada

verläuft. 15m von dieser Stelle entfernt führt rechts steil ein Hirtenpfad den Berg hoch. Eine kleine Steinpyramide zeigt den Weg an (siehe Wegmarkierung). Folgen Sie dem Pfad, der durch die Büsche schlängelt. Überall, wo er nicht klar erkennbar ist, finden Sie Wegmarkierungen mit roter Farbe oder Poseidonschilder an den Bäumen und Büschen. Die Wegrichtung wechselt von Norden nach Westen und kommt schließlich auf offenes Land, wo sich große Felsen zu Ihrer Rechten befinden. Nach einer Weile führt die Route zu einem Bauernhof. Gehen Sie zwischen den beiden Gebäuden hindurch zu einem Weg, der Sie nach 200m rechts auf die Hauptstraße führt. Überqueren Sie die Straße und gehen Sie weiter auf einem Feldweg in das Dorf Olympiada hinein. Nach weiteren 200m erscheint eine Kreuzung. Biegen Sie rechts ab und watten Sie nach 100m durch eine Furt über das ausbetonierte Flußbett. Der Weg biegt nach rechts ab und folgt dem Flußbett entlang bis zu einer Asphaltstraße an einer Brücke. Gehen Sie weiter geradeaus über die Straße hinweg Richtung Strand, der geradeaus vor Ihnen liegt. Dort angelangt biegen Sie rechts an der Taverne ab und gehen an den Geschäften vorbei zum Parkplatz zurück.

TAXI

This page will help you to book a taxi in a village, where you cannot find someone who speaks English. Just fill in the spaces with the time and place, where you want to be picked up and show it to the landlord in a local taverne or at a *periptero* (small kiosk, you find in Halkidiki on every village square).
(The place names can be written in Latin characters)

For your information : the translation of the Greek sentence in English is:
Can you help me, please?
We will make a walk from ....to.................
We would like to arrange a taxi, that picks us up at ....(hour) from..........
for .... persons.
Will you book that taxi for us? Thank you very much!

Diese Seite hilft Ihnen in einem Dorf ein Taxi zu bestellen, wenn Sie einmal niemanden finden der Deutsch oder Englisch spricht. Füllen Sie einfach in die Leerstellen die Uhrzeit ein, zu der Sie abgeholt werden wollen und den Ort, an dem Sie abgeholt werden wollen und zeigen Sie es in der örtlichen Taverne oder einem Periptero (kleiner Verkaufsstand, findet man am Hauptplatz in jedem Ort der Chalkidiki) dem Wirt oder Verkäufer. (Die Ortsnamen können Sie in lateinischen Buchstaben einfügen).
Hier als Information für Sie die deutsche Übersetzung des Satzes.
Können Sie mir bitte helfen?
Unsere Gruppe will eine Wanderung von................ nach.........unternehmen. Wir brauchen um........... Uhr ein Taxi, daß uns in........ abholt. Wir sind .....Personen. Können Sie bitte das Taxi für uns bestellen?
Herzlichen Dank!

Μπορείτε παρακαλώ να μας βοηθήσετε;
Η παρέα μας θέλει να περπατήσει από ....
έως .... Χρειαζόμαστε ένα ταξί
στις .... η ώρα, να μας παραλάβει από ....
Είμαστε ....άτομα.
Μπορείτε παρακαλώ να καλέσετε αυτό το ταξί;

Ευχαριστούμε πολύ!